P7-ESN-667

Islam: A Very Short Introduction

VERY SHORT INTRODUCTIONS are for anyone wanting a stimulating and accessible way in to a new subject. They are written by experts, and have been published in more than 25 languages worldwide.

The series began in 1995, and now represents a wide variety of topics in history, philosophy, religion, science, and the humanities. Over the next few years it will grow to a library of around 200 volumes – a Very Short Introduction to everything from ancient Egypt and Indian philosophy to conceptual art and cosmology.

Very Short Introductions available now:

Available soon:

For more information visit our web site

www.oup.co.uk/vsi

Malise Ruthven

ISLAM

A Very Short Introduction

OXFORD
UNIVERSITY PRESS

OXFORD

UNIVERSITY PRESS

Great Clarendon Street, Oxford OX2 6DP

Oxford University Press is a department of the University of Oxford.
It furthers the University's objective of excellence in research, scholarship,
and education by publishing worldwide in

Oxford New York

Auckland Bangkok Buenos Aires Cape Town Chennai
Dar es Salaam Delhi Hong Kong Istanbul Karachi Kolkata
Kuala Lumpur Madrid Melbourne Mexico City Mumbai Nairobi
São Paulo Shanghai Taipei Tokyo Toronto

Oxford is a registered trade mark of Oxford University Press
in the UK and in certain other countries

Published in the United States
by Oxford University Press Inc., New York

British Library Cataloguing in Publication Data

Data available

Library of Congress Cataloging in Publication Data
Ruthven, Malise.
Islam / Malise Ruthven.
Includes bibliographical references and index.
1. Islam. I. Title.
BP161.2.R86 1997   297—dc21   97-25616

ISBN 0-19-285389-9

9 10 8

Typeset by RefineCatch Ltd, Bungay, Suffolk
Printed in Great Britain by
TJ International Ltd., Padstow, Cornwall

Preface

To write a 'Very Short Introduction' to the religion of approximately one-fifth of the human family has been a daunting assignment. Brevity depends on selection, and selection on exclusion. Given the vast range of human societies contained under the label 'Islamic', any process of selection or exclusion must also entail distortion. In choosing to focus on certain topics at the expense of others, I am conscious of following my own instincts and prejudices. Professionally I am a journalist turned academic, and I have drawn on both disciplines in the book. The journalist in me has an eye on newspaper headlines. Aware that 'Islam' is seen by many as a hostile force, a possible replacement for communism as the main ideological challenge to post-Enlightenment liberalism, I have given more space to Islamic politics than some would say the subject warrants. The same might be said of my chapter on women and the family, a controversial subject that looms large in news coverage of the Islamic world. At the same time, the academic in me has tried to eschew the stereotypes or facile generalizations that usually accompany the treatment of these controversial topics in the media.

Early drafts of the text, or parts of it, have been read by my colleague James Thrower and by the academic readers consulted by Oxford University Press. My thanks to them for many suggestions for improvements which I have tried to incorporate in the final draft. Deniz Kandiyoti read an early draft of Chapter Five, and I have incorporated as many of her valuable insights and suggestions as possible. My thanks for her trouble at a busy time of the year. Due to the constraints of time, none of these readers has been shown the final draft, so the usual disclaimer that none is responsible for remaining errors, omissions, and over-simplifications must be made with more than usual force. I am solely responsible for the contents of this book.

Some of the material in Chapter Six has appeared in different guise in *The Middle East and North Africa*, published by Europa Publications; the *Muslim Almanac*, edited by Azim Nanji (Gale Research Inc.); and in the *London Review of Books*.

Contents

List of Illustrations

List of Maps

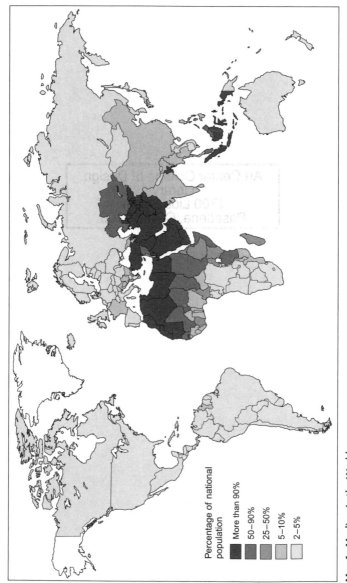

Percentage of national population

- More than 90%
- 50–90%
- 25–50%
- 5–10%
- 2–5%

Map 1. Muslims in the World.

Map 2. The Rise and Spread of Islam.

Expansion of Islam 632–44

Expansion of Islam 644–750

| 0 | 500 | 1000 km |
| 0 | 250 | 500 miles |

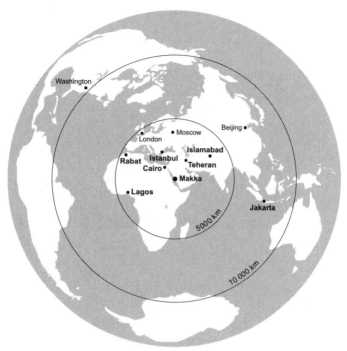

Map 3. A Makka-centric World.

Chapter 1

Islam, Muslims, and Islamism

Open almost any newspaper, turn on the radio or television, and there will be stories about Islam. Many of these stories will be accompanied by images of violence – as in Kashmir, Bosnia, Algeria, or Palestine. The vision of Islam emerging from newspapers and television screens is often that of a hard, uncompromising faith whose adherents will resort to violence in defence of their principles or in order to impose their will on others. Yet for those more familiar with Muslims and their traditions, the image of 'militant Islam' lies at odds with a faith that most of its adherents – who number, perhaps, a billion world-wide – would regard as no less pacific in temper than Buddhism or Christianity. The word Islam, in Arabic, means 'self-surrender'; it is closely related, etymologically to *salaam*, the word for peace. The universal greeting with which Muslims address each other, and foreigners, is *as salaam 'alaikum* – Peace Be Upon You.

The image of militancy, in the eyes of many Muslims, is a distortion by the Western media. There are solid grounds for this view. In an age of sound-bites and newspaper agendas driven by tabloid headlines, the lives and values of peace-loving majorities are inevitably obscured by the attention-seeking acts of the noisy minorities. The news media act like a distorting mirror at a fairground, exaggerating the militancy of the few while minimizing the quietism or indifference of the many.

These are not merely abstract reflections. The cumulative effect of distorted public perceptions feeds into the policy-making process. Samuel Huntington, an influential Harvard professor, states that 'Islam has bloody borders'. He predicts a 'clash of civilizations' between 'Islam', the 'West', and a revitalized Confucian China as the most likely scenario of global conflict following the collapse of Marxism-Leninism. His sentiments are often reciprocated: the word *gharb* in Arabic and other Muslim languages, as well as meaning 'west', shares the same root as *gharib*, meaning strange, outlandish, alien. Fuelled by atavistic notions of each as the hostile 'other' – motifs that stretch back to the Crusades – such predictions can all too easily become self-fulfilling. A policy of confrontation or containment, predicated on the notion that 'Islam' constitutes a 'threat' to the New World Order, could indeed strengthen those very political forces in the Islamic world that bark loudest in their hostility to the West. 'The myth of confrontation', writes Fred Halliday, a perceptive observer of international affairs, 'is sustained from two apparently contradictory sides – from the camp of those, mainly in the West, seeking to turn the Muslim world into another enemy, and from those within the Islamic countries who advocate confrontation with the non-Muslim, particularly Western, world.'

Defining Islam is far from a simple matter. Using Western categories that may be alien to Muslim perceptions, we may state from the start that Islam may be both a religious faith and a political ideology; it is also, in some contexts, a mark of personal and group identity. These three definitions neither exclude nor include each other.

Islam as Identity

'Islam' in Arabic is a verbal noun, meaning self-surrender to God as revealed through the message and life of his Prophet, Muhammad. In its primary meaning (for example, as employed in the Quran and other foundational texts) the word Muslim refers to one who so surrenders him- or herself (from the active participle of the verb *aslama*, to surrender oneself). There is, however, a secondary meaning to 'Muslim' which may shade into the first. A Muslim is one born to a Muslim father who takes on his or her parent's confessional identity without necessarily subscribing to the beliefs and practices of the faith, just as a Jew may define him- or herself as 'Jewish' without observing the Halacha. In non-Muslim societies such Muslims may subscribe to, and be vested with, secular identities. The Muslims of Bosnia, descendants of Slavs who converted to Islam under Ottoman rule, are not always noted for attendance at prayer, abstention from alcohol, seclusion of women, and other social practices associated with believing Muslims in other parts of the world. They were officially designated as Muslims to distinguish them from (Orthodox) Serbs and (Catholic) Croats under the former Yugoslavian communist regime. The label 'Muslim' indicates their ethnicity and group allegiance, but not necessarily their religious beliefs. In this limited context (which may also apply to other Muslim minorities in Europe and Asia) there may be no necessary contradiction between being Muslim and being atheist or agnostic, just as there are Jewish atheists and Jewish agnostics. The word Christian, by contrast, has in normal usage come to imply a strictly confessional affiliation: a 'Christian atheist' – though occasionally employed by avant-garde theologians – sounds to most people like a contradiction in terms, although we can still speak of Western culture as predominantly Christian. It should be noted, however, that this secular definition of 'Muslim' (sometimes the terms 'cultural Muslim' or 'nominal Muslim' are used) is very far from being uncontested. Just as fundamentalist Christians in America have reappropriated the term 'Christian' to apply exclusively to those who share their particular (usually narrow) versions of the faith, so modern Muslim activists have tended to redraw the boundaries between themselves and other Muslims who do not share their views, in extreme cases going so far as to designate the latter as 'infidels'. Generally there is little consistency in the way such labels are applied. Where Muslims, however secular or 'cultural', are beleaguered, as in Bosnia, a rhetorical generosity will include them among the

3

believers. Where, as in Egypt, a secular-minded majority may opt to collaborate with a government perceived by its critics as too secular, such non-observant Muslims may find themselves tarred with the 'infidel' brush. The words 'Islam' and 'Muslim' are disputed territory everywhere.

Islam as Political Ideology

The word 'fundamentalist' has passed into English usage to describe those Muslims who seek by whatever means to restore or establish an Islamic state. According to this view it is the task of the Islamic state to enforce obedience to the revealed law of Islam – the Shariʿa. The term 'fundamentalist' is problematic, because of its Christian origins: fundamentalism was originally a movement directed against liberal or modernist theology as taught in American Protestant seminaries, in particular those teachings that questioned literal understandings of such supernatural events as six-day creation, the virgin birth, and the physical resurrection and imminent return of Christ. Muslim writers and ideologists described as 'fundamentalist' have all adopted some modernistic and allegorical interpretations of the Quran, while virtually all believing Muslims – not just those described as 'fundamentalists' – see the Quran as the eternal unmediated Word of God. The focus for those seeking to defend Islam against what they see as the corrupting effects of modern secularism and the 'West' is *action* rather than *belief*. This agenda, however novel its methods of application (including the adoption of terrorist methods), generally accords with long-established historical patterns. Throughout history Islamic rectitude has tended to be defined in relation to practice rather than doctrine. Muslims who dissented from the majority on issues of leadership or theology were usually tolerated provided their social behaviour conformed to generally accepted standards. It is in enforcing behavioural conformity (ortho*praxy*) rather than doctrinal conformity (ortho*doxy*) that Muslim radicals or activists look to a 'restoration' of Islamic law backed by the power of the state.

4

The means adopted towards achieving this end, however, may vary according to the political institutions of the country concerned. In some countries, such as Jordan, Muslim radicals sit as parliamentary representatives. In Algeria and to a lesser extent Egypt, they are engaged in an armed conflict with the state. In Sudan and formerly in Pakistan, they have exercised power on the backs of military dictatorships. In Iran they operate under a hybrid system, sitting as parliamentary representatives chosen from a restricted list of like-minded candidates. However, even when, as in Jordan, the democratic option may be adopted as a means to an end, democracy as such may be rejected. Most Muslims belonging to the militant tendency challenge the fundamentals of the international order: in the terms of one of their most influential mentors, Sayyid Abul 'Ala Maududi (1903–79), they aim to replace the sovereignty of the people expressed through parliamentary legislation, with the 'sovereignty of God' as revealed, in its perfection and finality, through the Shari'a.

Critics of this approach – and there are many – direct their fire at two of its arguments. Historically, they point out that no Islamic society, even during the high tide of Islamic civilization, was governed exclusively according to Islamic law. There was always a gap between the theoretical formulations of the jurists and the *de facto* exercise of political power. Moreover, given the enormous cultural and geographical differences between Muslim societies, Islamic law was everywhere supplemented by local customary laws. In legal-historical terms, the Shari'a was never a reality.

The second, more damaging, criticism directed at those who insist on politicizing Islam, is misrepresentation. Far from being exclusively 'Islamic', the ideology or ideologies being advanced are really hybrids mixing Islamic concepts with twentieth-century ideas, liberal and totalitarian. The founders of modern political Islam – Maududi, Sayyid Qutb (1906–66), and the Ayatollah Khomeini (1902–89) – were profoundly influenced by the Western political and intellectual cultures they professed to oppose. Thus Maududi's critique of Western materialism and moral decadence was informed by fascist attacks on democracy and an admiration for the dictators of the 1930s. Qutb's call for action against barbarism (*jahiliya*), far from being based on 'traditional' Islam, is thoroughly modern in its espousal of an 'existentialist', action-oriented commitment, while his claim that democracy and social justice have Islamic origins is considered by some to be spurious, based on an ahistorical reading of Islam's sacred texts. (Even the virulent anti-Semitism he adopted in the wake of the Arab–Israeli conflict is partly imported, based on the uncritical adoption of European ideas.) Likewise the 'Islamic' Constitution of Iran, introduced by Khomeini in 1979, is a mixture of Western and Islamic forms, not an 'Islamic' constitution as such. Far from being subject to Islamic law, Khomeini made it clear that the Islamic state, as successor to the Prophet Muhammad, had the power to override Islamic law, even in such fundamentals of the faith as prayer, fasting, and pilgrimage.

In the view of political Islam's numerous critics, Muslim and non-Muslim, Islam as religion should be distinguished from Islam as political ideology. To call the latter 'fundamentalism' is not only misleading; it makes a gratuitous concession to the advocates of political Islam by implying that the defence of Islam's 'fundamentals' invariably demands political action. Muslims who contest this view argue that so long as a government does not prevent the believer from carrying out his or her religious duties, it cannot be described as un- or anti-Islamic.

Islam as Faith

The classical authorities made a distinction between *islam* as professed by the Muslim on the one hand, and *iman* or faith of the *mumin* (believer) on the other. In the original wars that united the Arabian peninsula (see Chapter 2) the self-surrender or submission to God, however sincere, occurred through the exterior agencies of the Prophet and his followers. The Quran alludes to an incident when a group of bedouin Arabs claim to have become believers and are told by God through the Prophet: 'You have not [yet] attained to faith; you should [rather] say: "We have [outwardly] surrendered" for [true] faith has not yet entered your hearts' (Quran 49: 14)*. Faith would follow surrender to the Muslim Prophet, conviction the appeal of his divine charisma. In due course the degree of conviction required of the believer became the subject of theological debate. The puritanical Kharijis (Seceders) cast their net very narrowly, denying grave sinners the right to call themselves Muslims. The same puritanical tendency has been revived by militant groups today, who exclude lax or nominal Muslims from their definition of the *umma*, the world-wide community of believers. The Kharijis' opponents, known as the Murji'a, allowed that virtually anyone could be considered a Muslim so long as they proclaimed the *shahada*, the public declaration of faith enshrined in the formula 'There is no god but God; Muhammad is the Messenger of God'. Most of the classical authorities took the broader view. Abu Hanifa, whose name was given to one of the four legal schools of Sunni Islam, stated that 'those who face in the direction of Makka at prayer are true believers and no act of theirs can remove them from the faith'. In time a majority of Muslims came to accept the view that *iman* and *islam* represented the internal and external aspects of religious commitment, faith and works. The exoteric or 'outward' manifestations of the faith, through observance of ritual and adherence to the Shari'a law, defined the Muslim *vis-à-vis* the outside world; but many came to consider that true piety was to be found in esoteric dimensions of the faith known only to a spiritual élite. In the absence of a formally constituted hierarchy or 'church', members of this élite were known by their knowledge of the religious disciplines and their command of spiritual or ascetical practices not normally acquired by the majority. Among the Shi'i minority, the spiritual élite is characterized by its proximity in kinship to the Prophet Muhammad and his family. Esotericism, including the exploration of hidden meanings in scripture and secret or unconventional religious practices, became the hallmark of movements that dissented from the majority politically or in religious style. The broadly tolerant view that

Islam, Muslims, and Islamism

7

determined Islam exoterically, by reference to *islam* as distinct from *iman*, allowed a great variety of spiritual growths to flourish without scandal. Although seekers after political power tended to wrap themselves in religious symbols just as avidly as they did in the West in pre-modern times, with polemicists routinely accusing each other of heresy, the history of Islam, however scarred by violence, is remarkably free from the forms of religious intolerance that found expression in the medieval and Spanish inquisitions. In modern times the sense of inner commitment linking the believer to God in a personal relationship that may transcend the external imperatives of ritual and law has, despite appearances to the contrary, greatly assisted the privatization and secularization of the faith.

No religion could prosper and survive, as Islam has prospered and survived into modern times, if it were exclusively bound by the outward or exoteric forms of observance. No less than other successful modern religions Islam contains a rich repertoire of concepts, symbols, and spiritual disciplines through which believers maintain their identities and sense of being in the world, their sense of being in contact with God. The crisis many Muslims are facing in adjusting to the realities of the contemporary world is not the result of some inherent lack of flexibility in the realm of ideas. Historically Islam has shown enormous adaptability in accommodating different cultural systems within its overarching framework: the Abrahamic 'family' of western Asian monotheism that includes Judaism and Christianity as well as Islam.

The crisis of modern Islam – and few would deny that such a crisis exists – is not so much a 'spiritual crisis' as a crisis of authority – political, intellectual, and legal as well as spiritual. The 'best community' ordained by God for 'enjoining what is right and forbidding what is wrong' – a community that successfully conducted its own affairs for centuries, without external interference – demands leadership. Yet outside the Shi'i minority tradition, a leadership commanding universal support is conspicuously absent.

Institutional Leadership

There is no 'church' in Islam, no formally instituted body empowered to supervise or dictate the religious agenda, to articulate an 'official' Islamic view comparable to that of the Papacy or the appointed or elected leadership of Protestant denominations. With the collapse of the Islamic superstate that lasted barely two centuries after the death of the Prophet Muhammad, religious authority was entrusted to the *ulama* (sing.: *'alim*, 'learned man'), a class of scholars, whose role as guardians and interpreters of the tradition is much closer to that of the rabbis in Judaism than that of a Christian priesthood. They did not exercise political power but acted as a break on the power of the rulers, the *sultans* ('authorities') and *amirs* ('commanders'), most of whom came to power by force of arms, interpreting and administering the divine law according to complex rules developed in the academies. The most prestigious of these academies, Al-Azhar in Cairo, was founded in 971 CE and claims to be the oldest university in the world. Though its rector – the Shaikh al-Azhar – enjoys pre-eminence among the Sunni *ulama*, his opinions are not binding on his peers; similarly, though all Muslim governments will appoint an official *mufti*, an *'alim* possessed of the authority to deliver legal judgments on a variety of issues, his opinions are purely consultative unless given effect in a court judgment by a *qadi*, a judge. It is the ruler who appoints the judge, so the implementation of the religious law, but not its interpretation, is under state control. Mass education policies undertaken by most post-colonial governments have led to a relative decline in the prestige and authority of the *ulama* as graduates with mainly secular educational backgrounds forge their own interpretations of Islam's sacred texts, short-circuiting the traditional body of scholarship. Alternatively, in countries which have been less subject to modernizing influences, such as Afghanistan or the rural parts of Pakistan, *ulama* or aspiring *ulama* may seek to exercise power directly, oblivious of the modern world's complex realities. In either case, the crisis of intellectual authority is ultimately the same: the traditionally trained *ulama* have failed to incorporate contemporary modernist or reformist thinking into their discourse. Activists seeking to 'Islamize' their societies, bringing them more closely into line with what they perceive to be Islamic law, ignore the centuries of nuanced and qualifying scholarship by which the ʿulama in the past reconciled the demands of the divine law with the realities of political power and the exigencies of everyday life.

Legal Modernization

That there is a serious gap between the requirements of Islamic law and the actual legal practice of most Muslim majority states is arguably a matter of perception rather than reality. Earlier this century a great modern jurist, ʿAbd al-Razzaq Sanhuri, worked hard to reconcile Islamic law with the Western systems of law introduced under the colonial and post-colonial governments of Muslim states. Radical Muslims who demand that the Shariʿa be 'restored' in its entirety are not acknowledging the extent to which this work, which was incorporated into the domestic legislation of many Muslim states, found common ground between formerly competing legal systems. In practice, demands for the 'restoration' of the Shariʿa tend to focus on particular aspects of the criminal law, notably the corporal punishments specified in the Quran and early Muslim tradition for sexual offences and certain categories of theft. In some parts of the world the *hudud* penalties (according to which transgressions of the 'limits' or 'boundaries' prescribed by God in the Quran are given specified punishments such as amputation for theft or flogging for sexual relations outside marriage) have acquired a symbolic significance precisely because they are seen to confront licentious attitudes deemed to have been inspired by a 'decadent' West. Less controversially, the traditional Islamic ban on *riba*, understood as all forms of money loaned at interest, has led to some creative experiments in financial risk-sharing and equity participation by Islamic banks, which try to apportion the risks undertaken by lenders and borrowers more equitably than the conventional banking system does. Here the Islamic concern for equity in business relationships offers a challenge to a post-Christian world where corporate power often flourishes at the expense of the individual or family needs. Generally, however, demands for the 'restoration' of the Shari'a are part of what the progressivist Algerian-born scholar Muhammad Arkoun calls the 'social imaginary' of Muslims – the 'collection of images' held within a culture about itself or other cultures, images that tend to preclude analysis and objective self-reflection while feeding fantasies based on romantic, ahistorical visions of the past.

Successes and Failures of the Islamic State

The social imaginary, or better, perhaps social *memory*, lies at the heart of the collective aspirations which hark back to a golden age when *dar al-islam* (the sphere of Islam, distinguished in Islamic legal tradition from *dar al-harb*, the sphere of war) was still expanding and Muslim communities excelled in all the arts of civilization. No one need doubt that, at the level of civilization, an unprecedented degree of knowledge, excellence and sophistication was achieved in *dar al-islam* several centuries before the Renaissance occurred in Europe, or that, as many scholars have noted, much of the groundwork for the scientific and philosophical thought that would flourish in the West was laid in Muslim lands. A short introductory text such as this cannot hope to even hint at the achievements of Muslims in the areas in which they excelled – architecture and design, metalwork and ceramics, poetry and philosophy, as well as the 'harder' sciences including mathematics, optics, astronomy, and medicine. Apart from the restrictions of space, however, there remains the thorny question of how far such cultural achievements are 'Islamic' in the sense that they can be attributed directly or even indirectly to the religion of Islam, and how far they build on and carry forward the achievements of preceding (mainly Greek and Persian) civilizations. The American historian Marshall Hodgson distinguished between 'Islamic' (pertaining to the religion) and what he termed 'Islamicate' (pertaining to the broader cultural and societal frame of which the religion is part, and over which it may be said to preside). The distinction is a useful one, even though it has not been widely adopted, and probably raises as many questions as it answers.

More central to the concerns of this essay are the problems of authority and power. Islamdom, like Christendom, its historical rival, aspires to universality. The failure of *dar al-islam* to maintain its initial momentum and to incorporate the globe within its domain hardly requires explanation, given the limitations of pre-modern technologies: the vastness of the territories encompassed by the Arabs in the first wave of invasions are astonishing enough in an era when the maximum distance a human being could travel (under the most favourable conditions) would have been no more than thirty or forty miles per day. The very speed and range of the initial expansion, however, were the source of political problems that remain unresolved after thirteen centuries. Islam initially expanded on the wings of tribalism. Submission to 'God and his Prophet' was, in the first instance, submission to a victorious bedouin army. From the first, the message of social justice and the equality of men (and, more problematically, of women) before God, as conveyed in Muhammad's preaching and preserved in the Quran, came up against the realities of tribal and dynastic power. The civil wars that occurred within a generation of the Prophet's death in 632, the split between Sunni and Shiʿa, the collapse of the Arab empire, and the political fragmentation that occurred in its wake – all of these historical events bear witness to an unfulfilled project: the establishment of divine government on earth.

In the absence of church or priesthood, the execution of the project was left to the uncertainties of lay enthusiasts. Leadership was assumed by two elements, often in contradiction to each other. On one side it passed to the tribal leaders for whom Islam (sometimes in its most heterodox, messianic versions) became the cement of tribal solidarity, the ideological force which directed energies previously consumed in internecine struggles outwards towards conquest; on the other to the ʿulama, the lay interpreters of the law, respected guardians of the tradition, but possessing no executive powers and reliant on outsiders, sometimes brought in as slaves from distant regions, to carry out God's commands. An uneasy compromise between these two agencies, the military rulers and the *ulama*, produced a rough and ready constitutional balance in what has been called an 'international civilization', the first perhaps, in history. As Marshall Hodgson argued with passion and conviction, the 'Venture of Islam' did much to satisfy the needs of peoples in the urban regions lying between the Nile and Oxus rivers by facilitating the emergence of a common trading area based on the shared values of justice and fair dealings under God.

This historical achievement (which may without too much distortion appear as a golden age in the social memory of Muslims) was counter-balanced by a conspicuous failure at the level of power politics. After its initial expansion, the Arab empire imploded. Islam's central institution, the caliphate, at first contested by rival factions was gradually drained of legitimacy, as the caliph, the 'shadow of God on earth' became the prisoner of palace guards recruited from the tribes. The social memory focuses on several towering caliphal figures; the Four Rightly-Guided Caliphs – Abu Bakr (r.632–4), 'Umar (634–44), 'Uthman, and 'Ali (656–61); and the great Harun al-Rashid (786–809), the ideal monarch immortalized in the stories of the *Thousand and One Nights*, when the Arab empire was at its height. What social memory cannot address, of course, is the essential ambiguity of the caliphate. Scholars are still debating whether the early caliphate was a religious or political office, or a combination of both, and if so, in what proportions. The term is as ambiguous as the office it describes. In the Quran it is applied to Adam, the first man and God's vice-regent, and to David, a prophet who is also a king. The office as such emerged spontaneously after the death of the Prophet, who left no clear successor or rules for the succession. The first four caliphs succeeded by acclamation, in accordance with tribal custom. Some jurists argued that thereafter the true caliphate ceased, and that subsequent caliphs were merely monarchs or kings. In orthodox writings the title caliph generally means deputy or successor to the Prophet Muhammad (as in *khalifat rasul Allah* – deputy to the Messenger of God). Early Umayyad caliphs and some of the ʿAbbasids who supplanted them employed the title *khalifat Allah* – deputy or vice-regent of God (as did some later Muslim sovereigns, such as the Sultan of Jogjakarta in Java). It seems clear that until the middle of the ninth century the caliph exercised spiritual functions in addition to his political ones, enforcing religious conformity. After a populist reaction against efforts by the Caliph al-Mamun to impose what are sometimes described as rationalist doctrines on government officials, through the *mihna* or 'inquisition', the attempt at centralized control was abandoned, and guardianship of orthodoxy passed to the ʿ*ulama*.

The consequences of the caliphal debacle are far-reaching when the destiny of Islamic governance is compared with that of Christianity in the West, where the Church under generally vigorous Papal control retained a monopoly over Christian doctrine and the rituals that guaranteed salvation. Although the Catholic monopoly was eventually broken, the Church's long hegemony effected social transformations that transcended the bonds of kinship. The occidental state merged as the Church – the ideal corporation embodying the person of Christ – gave birth to secular offspring in the shape of cities and other public entities. The Islamic state, by contrast, never fully transcended its tribal matrix. The implosion of the Arab empire compounded the Caliph's failure to enforce religious conformity. Apart from the Shiʿa, who held to the idea of a transcendent spiritual authority, the lack of any central institution in Islam charged with the task of religious governance impeded the emergence of its counterweight in the shape of the secular state. The law developed separately from the agencies entrusted with its enforcement, and so military-tribal rule became the norm. As Patricia Crone and Martin Hinds have argued, 'a ruler who has no say at all in the definition of the law by which his subjects have chosen to live cannot rule those subjects in any but a purely military sense'. To perpetuate itself, such a state must be manned by outsiders, and it is as outsiders, not as representatives of the community, that the rulers are obeyed. Although there was an element of consensus in this relationship, there was also, as Crone and Hinds point out, 'a total lack of institutional machinery behind [it] . . . The state was thus something which sat on top of society, not something which was rooted in it: and given that there was minimal interaction between the two, there was also minimal political development: dynasties came and went, but it was only the dynasties that changed.' This formulation may exaggerate the degree of political immobility in Muslim states, but it makes an important point about the relationship between the state and civil society in Muslim lands prior to the modern period (roughly from the nineteenth century), when Muslim rulers became aware of the need to introduce changes into their societies in order to face the military and economic challenges posed by the West.

A Religious Awakening?

However much the experts may disagree on its long-term political implications, the resurgence of Islamic observance in daily life – increasing attendance at mosque, observance of fasting during Ramadan, a proliferation of religious publications in print and audio-visual media, and increasing emphasis on 'Islamic dress' in many parts of the world, especially for women – is undeniable. Two of the factors most frequently cited in explanation are the unprecedented scale of urbanization and the failure of the post-colonial state to deliver on its promises. Migration to the cities means both the loss of village life, where extended family networks reinforce traditional social values, and exposure to modern urban life, with its Westernized customs. On the political level, the collapse of communism and the failure of Marxism to overcome the stigma of 'atheism' makes Islam seem an attractive ideological weapon against post-colonial regimes perceived as corrupt and authoritarian and sometimes tyrannical. In countries lacking effective democratic institutions the mosque and the network of activities surrounding it can enjoy a degree of immunity. If governments dare to close down 'rebel' mosques they confirm the charges of disbelief levelled against them by their opponents.

The explosion of information technology and particularly the revolution in audio-visual communication undercuts the authority of the literate élites, while exposing ever-growing numbers of people to transgressive and often salacious images created by the Western entertainment and advertising industries. In many countries an exponential leap in the rate of urbanization has decisively altered the cultural and demographic balance between urban and rural populations, creating a vast new proletariat of recently urbanized migrants susceptible to the messages of populist preachers and demagogues. In countries such as Egypt the Islamist political movements, through their welfare organizations, have been able to fill the gaps caused by government failure to deal with poverty and housing shortages as well as other social problems caused by over-rapid urbanization.

Or a Spiritual Vacuum?

In pre-modern times, before the colonial period, Islamic societies were bound together not only by family and clan solidarities, but by the mystical Sufi brotherhoods to which most adult male members in urban societies belonged (see Chapter 4). Although the Islamic revival has been accompanied to some degree by a revival of Sufi practices, the combined impact of the post-colonial nationalist struggle and the modernist movement led to a drastic decline of Sufism, seen by modernizers as a mark of 'backwardness' and by religious purists as tainted by heresy or, even worse, by paganism. Yet in the absence of a priesthood, the Sufi *shaikhs* ('old men'), *murshids* (spiritual guides), or *pirs* (as they are known in Persian- and Urdu-speaking lands) were a source of spiritual authority that complemented and sometimes exceeded the intellectual authority of the *'ulama*. Though some Sufi brotherhoods took a leading part in the anti-colonial struggles, others collaborated with the colonial authorities. The latter saw them as allies

16

against the modernists and reformers who pioneered the modern nationalist movements. Sufism with its 'vision of union and oneness', its ascetical other-worldly orientation, and its concern with the esoteric dimensions of the faith transcends the mundane particularities of politics, and the inevitably corrupting effects of power. Peter Von Sivers, a leading American scholar, links the rise of the modern political movements in Islam directly to the decline of Sufism, which many would see as the spiritual heart and soul of Islam. The exclusion of Sufism from the debate between secular-minded reformists and their religiously oriented opponents makes for an increasingly arid confrontation between violent extremes.

Conclusion: Islam and Islamism

The religious revival in modern Islam is a reflection of the pace of social and technological change in the Muslim world, particularly the disruptive effects of a rapid increase in urbanization. In this respect the causes are similar to those in Latin America and parts of sub-Saharan Africa where the late twentieth century has seen a massive increase in the activities of Protestant churches. However, the increase in Islamic observance evidenced by such indicators as prayer, fasting, and attendance at the Hajj, the annual pilgrimage to Makka, is inevitably associated with the political aspirations of Muslims, most of whom live in post-colonial states run by governments perceived as lacking in moral or spiritual authority. The rise of mass education and, increasingly, the appearance of audio-visual modes of communication has led to a decline in traditional sources of religious authority among both the 'ulama and the leadership of the Sufi brotherhoods. The gap has been filled by a variety of movements and leaders, all of whom claim a religious legitimacy for their acts. There are many historical precedents for movements of religious revival challenging and sometimes taking power in Islamic countries before the colonial and post-colonial international order brought most of the world into its economic and cultural orbit.

1. The Ka'ba, the cube-shaped temple at the centre of the Noble Sanctuary in Makka. Pilgrims circumambulate the Ka'ba and Muslims everywhere pray in its direction. The Kiswa or black silk covering is replaced every year.

2. The Hajj terminal, King ʿAbdul ʿAziz International Airport near Jedda, Saudi Arabia. The vast tented halls constructed from insulated fabrics developed in space research can accommodate pilgrims at the rate of 5,000 per hour enhancing the accessibility and affordability of the Hajj.

It would be wrong to conclude from this, however, that contemporary Islamic political movements are no more than the latest examples of an age-old cyclical pattern. The revivalist movements which often seem to dominate the headlines are modern, not just in their methods, which may include sophisticated techniques of organization as well as the use of guns, rockets, and bombs. They are modern in that they have absorbed into a 'traditional' Islamic discourse many ideas imported from outside the Islamic intellectual tradition. The decline in traditional forms of spirituality represented by the Sufi brotherhoods has been accompanied by the 'ideologization' of Islam at the political level, the construction of a political ideology using some symbols culled from the historical repertoire of Islam, to the exclusion of others. This ideology, sometimes referred to as 'Islamic fundamentalism', is better described as *Islamism*: the Latin suffix attached to the Arabic original more accurately expresses the relationship between the pre-existing reality (in this case a religion) and its translation into a political ideology, just as communism ideologizes the reality of the commune, socialism the social, and fascism the ancient symbol of Roman consular authority. Islamism is not Islam. Though the lines dividing them are frequently blurred, it is important to distinguish between them.

Chapter 2
The Quran and the Prophet

Earlier this century Muslims were often referred to as Muhammadans, the religion of Islam as Muhammadanism. That the usage has now been abandoned is partly a reflection of the political changes that have occurred since the time when most of the Islamic world was under European colonial rule. Europeans, especially in south Asia, saw the respect Muslims accord their Prophet as tantamount to worship. Muslims did not usually refer to themselves as Muhammadans (except as a descriptive term when addressing Europeans), because to do so would seem to imply that they worshipped Muhammad as Christians worshipped Christ. For orthodox Muslims such an implication was highly offensive. Muslims worship God, not Muhammad. The Messenger was a prophet, not a deity or divine avatar. To suggest otherwise would be to breach the boundary between God and humankind, the creator and his creation. Theologically maintenance of that boundary is the central article of the Islamic faith. 'There is no god but God. Muhammad is the Messenger of God.'

That is not to say that Muhammad is in any sense ordinary, or that his role is less central to the formation of Islam than Christ's is to that of Christianity. Arguably, the reverse applies. Because of the voluminous nature of the Islamic canon there are many more actions, thoughts, and sayings attributed to Muhammad than there are to Jesus. The difference lies not in his historical influence or the degree of fascination exercised over the minds of his followers, but rather in the different status accorded to his utterances. Muslims of all persuasions distinguish between those sayings attributed to Muhammad in his capacity as a prophet or divine revelator – utterances that are collected in the Quran (in its original meaning, the 'Recitation'); and those of a lesser status recorded by his contemporaries in a secondary body of scripture known as the Hadiths ('Traditions'). Though some degree of controversy surrounds both categories, this difference of status is something on which Muslim and non-Muslim commentators are generally agreed.

The Quran

For the vast majority of Muslims the Quran is the speech of God, dictated without human editing. It is more than a sacred text such as is found in other traditions. Following the Mu'tazili controversy (see pp. 58–9 below), the Quran came to be regarded as 'uncreated', hence coextensive with God. As Wilfred Cantwell-Smith observes, it occupies for believing Muslims the position Christ has for Christians. A Muslim should not handle the text unless he or she is in a state of ritual purity. The exact pronunciation is as important as the meanings; unlike most Arabic texts, the Quranic script is supplied with the short vowel-sign to ensure the greatest degree of oral accuracy. Readings are preceded by the phrase 'I take refuge with God from Satan, the accursed one', and followed by 'God Almighty has spoken truly!' The opening and closing formulae establish 'a sort of verbal ritual enclosure or sanctuary around the recited text, preserving it from evil promptings or insincerity'. Certain verses are credited with curative powers: for example, the first sura or chapter, known as the Opening, is good for scorpion bites; the last two (suras 113 and 114) are good for various illnesses.

Much scholarly argument surrounds the assemblage of the text. Most non-Muslim scholars, with a few exceptions, accept that the written book contains a record of the divine utterances made by Muhammad in the course of his prophetic ministry starting around 610 CE and ending

with his death in 632. According to various traditions, Muhammad fell
into a trance-like state when revelations came to him. These traditions
are consistent with accounts of revelations received by more recent
prophets, such as Joseph Smith Jr., the founder of Mormonism, whose
prophetic utterances are contained in the scripture known as *Doctrine
and Covenants*. Muslim historians are generally agreed that some
or all of these utterances, which are carefully distinguished from
Muhammad's 'normal' speech as recorded in the hadith literature,
were written down during his lifetime. Each of the four 'Rightly-Guided'
caliphs has been credited with initiating or forwarding the collection
of the text. However, the historians and traditionists are unanimous
that the official codex was adopted under the third Caliph 'Uthman
(r. 644–56). Variant readings were eventually destroyed, but not entirely
eliminated – a task made difficult by the condition of the earliest
Arabic writing, which lacks the diacritical points used to distinguish
consonants from each other. As the script evolved so the text became
standardized. The variant readings have been reduced to seven, each
of which is regarded as equally valid.

The book is organized into 114 suras (literally 'rows') or chapters,

The Fatiha

*'In the Name of God, the Merciful, the Compassionate
Praise belongs to God, the Lord of all Being,
the All-merciful, the All-compassionate,
Master of the Day of Doom.
Thee only we serve; to Thee alone we pray for succour.
Guide us in the straight path,
the path of those whom Thou hast blessed,
not of those against whom Thou art wrathful,
nor of those who are astray.'*
Quran 1: 1–7

The Quran encapsulated

'[The Fatiha] contains, in a condensed form, all the fundamental principles laid down in the Quran: the principle of God's oneness and uniqueness, of his being the originator and fosterer of the universe, the fount of all life-giving grace, the One to whom man is ultimately responsible, the only power that can really guide and help, the call to righteous *action* in the life of this world, . . . the principle of life after death and of the organic consequences of man's action and behaviour, . . . the principle of guidance through God's message-bearers . . . and, flowing from it, the principle of continuity of all true religions . . . ; and finally, the need for voluntary self-surrender to the will of the Supreme Being and, thus, for worshipping Him alone.'

Muhammad Asad, *The Message of the Quran* (1984), 1.

arranged approximately in order of length, with the shortest at the end and the longest near the beginning. The most important exception to this pattern is the first sura, the Fatiha or Opening, a seven-verse invocation repeated during the five prayers Muslims are required to perform every twenty-four hours. Sometimes called the 'Mother of the Book', the Fatiha is seen as the quintessence of Islam. It is in frequent use as a prayer.

In the subsequent suras the same fundamental message is repeated, elaborated, amplified, and illustrated with stories using the repertoire of Judaeo-Christian tradition with the addition of some distinctive Arabian elements. Adam and Noah, Abraham and Joseph, Moses and Jesus appear along with the Arabian prophets and sages – unknown to the Bible – Hud, Salih, and Luqman. The theology is an absolute and uncompromising monotheism. As in the Old Testament the prophets are sent to warn people against straying from the path of righteousness by worshipping false gods. Particularly heinous is the sin of *shirk* or

23

'associationism' by which God's majesty is compromised through contamination, as it were, by lesser deities. God's will, majesty, and creative power are continually stressed and celebrated. *Allah* – the Arabic word for God – includes the definite article. It means literally 'the god'. Rather than speculating fruitlessly about his attributes, humans are urged to acknowledge his presence and obey the moral laws and commands deemed to have been revealed to them through successive messengers or prophets. The last of these is Muhammad. God is both transcendent and immanent, the Lord of Creation and One who is nearer to an individual than his 'jugular vein'.

That it is God, rather than Muhammad, who speaks in the Quran is evident from the way many of the utterances are prefixed by the imperative 'Say!', addressed to Muhammad. God refers to himself in the first person singular and plural; but the Prophet is also addressed, apparently, by the Book itself and told about God as a third person. Many of these passages are clearer if they are understood to be spoken by angels or by the angel Gabriel. This is especially the case in passages occurring near the beginning of the book, but considered to belong to the later Medinese period of Muhammad's ministry – passages containing detailed prescriptions about marriage, inheritance, and punishment that represent the primary source of Islamic law.

What the Quran lacks for the reader familiar with the Bible or Hindu epics is a coherent narrative structure. Although there are some individual narratives – notably stories of the prophets, including the so-called 'punishment stories' detailing the direful fates meted out to those who reject God's messengers – the historical discourses are linked thematically rather than chronologically. The biblical narratives addressed to Christians and Jews are presented as reminders and reaffirmations of previous revelations, not as new revelations. Important differences of doctrine, however, emerge in these narratives. The most significant theological difference in terms of the historical development of Islam is the treatment of the Fall. Satan is punished for his refusal to bow down before

3. A page from the Quran: an example of Naskhi script. The text is Surat al-Nas (114): 'Say: "I take refuge with the Lord of men, the King of men, the God of men, from the evil of the slinking whisperer who whispers in the breasts of men, of jinn and men." '

God's mouthpiece

'Muhammad is the mouthpiece of the divine will, which is communicated to him by Gabriel, and thus, like a confidential official, he stands on the border-line between the king's court and the subjects. Subject he is always. Sometimes he receives messages to convey to the people, or receives commands or exhortations intended for them; sometimes he is directly addressed as the representative of the people, or he receives commands and exhortations intended for them; at other times special exhortations and directions for his own conduct are addressed to him; and at times he steps, as it were, across the line, and facing round upon the people conveys the divine commands and exhortations directly to them.'

W. M. Watt, *Bell's Introduction to the Quran* (Edinburgh, 1970), 67.

Adam; and though Adam sins, as in the biblical story, by eating of the forbidden fruit, he repents and is soon restored to favour as God's deputy or vice-regent (*khalifa*), the first prophet in the line of prophets that culminates in Muhammad. There is no doctrine of original sin here, no idea of vicarious atonement. Where there is no original sin, there is no redeemer: the Quranic Jesus is a prophet, born of a Virgin, but he is not the deity incarnate. Where there is neither incarnation nor redeemer, there can be no church, no 'bride' nor 'mystical body' of God. No Eternal Corporation is necessary to guarantee salvation. All that is required of humans is that they obey God's commands and use their intelligence in discerning truth from falsehood, using the Quran as their criterion (*furqan*). God reveals himself, not in a Person, but in what becomes a Text, the words of which are regarded by most Muslims as divine in themselves.

The verses into which the Quranic suras are divided are known in Arabic as *ayas* – the word means 'sign' and is frequently employed in the Quran

Signs and verses

'Each ayah of the Quran is also a sign – in the symbolic or semi-otic sense – that points to another level of reality that in turn reaffirms the message of revelation. The believer who seeks to develop a sense of the sacred must thus learn two distinct levels of "language" (*langue*) at the same time – the Arabic text of the Quran itself and the "language" of nature, which is also a mani-festation of the speech of God. God created the world as a book; his revelations descended to Earth and were compiled into a book; therefore the human being must learn to "read" the world as a book.'

Vincent J. Cornell in John L. Esposito (ed.), *Oxford Encyclopedia of the Modern Islamic World* (New York, 1995) iii. 388.

to demonstrate the existence of God. These 'signs', as well as referring to divine locutions, point to the evidences of God in nature. The theology of the Quran is thus suffused with what became known in Christian theology as the 'argument from design'. The act of reading is in itself an act of devotion.

Although Muhammad is mentioned by name on at least four occasions, there is almost nothing in the Quran, beyond the occasional hint, from which a biography of Muhammad or an account of his ministry can be inferred. In New Testament terms, it is as if the Epistles were preserved, without any of the four Gospels or Acts of the Apostles. The Quran 'is as little concerned with the events of the life of Muhammad as Paul was with the narrative life of Jesus'.

The style of the Quran is allusive and elliptical. It is addressed to people already familiar with much of the material it contains. Far from being self-explanatory, it can only be understood by reference to material *outside* itself. The very difficulties it presents as a historical source are a strong prima facie case for its authenticity. A work that had been subjected to any kind of redaction would surely show more signs of narrative coherence. One has the impression that Muhammad's words (those articulated in the prophetic mode, when he is supposed to have been possessed by the angel, or God) were regarded from the start as holy artefacts, distinct from his other utterances and worthy to be recorded and stored like sacred relics. Unlike the books of the Old and New Testaments, the Quran suggests itself as unedited 'raw material'. The narrative context in which it occurred – the career of Muhammad – was something that had to be reconstructed in order to approach its multiple meanings. Here, even to the sceptic, chronology conforms to theology. Just as 'God's speech' as delivered by the angel enjoys a higher ontological status than the speeches of the Prophet recorded in the hadith literature, so the Prophet's Life appears *after* the testimony of the Book. Far from Muhammad being the 'author' of the Quran, the Quran is, in a literary-historical sense, the 'author' of Muhammad.

Sira (*Biography*)

Muhammad the Prophet has achieved such eminence as a world-historical figure that it is difficult to conceive of him as having lived out his life in a cultural milieu without historical records, where history is wrapped in myth and historical facts are virtually out of reach. The events of his life, carefully reconstructed from hints and allusions in the Quran and from the oral testimonies of his companions and their successors, were written down more than a century after his death in dramatically different circumstances from those in which his life was lived. By then the victorious Arab tribes, under the banner of Islam, had broken out of the Arabian peninsula and conquered much of the civilized world, including Egypt, Palestine, Syria, Mesopotamia, and the highlands of Persia. Much more sophisticated cultures, Zoroastrian, Christian, and Jewish, had come under Arab dominion. Factional feuding had broken out between the tribes while the new cult of Allah and his

Arabian prophet faced criticism from the trained theological minds of the older religions.

The earliest Lives of the Prophet that have come down to us are both exegetical and apologetic in purpose. They serve to explain the 'occasions of revelation' – the particular circumstances in the Prophet's life when a verse or passage of the Quran 'came down'. Their treatment of events may be influenced by hindsight or by a retrospective colouring designed to bolster the claims of one of the factions competing for power. They contain a good deal of material of a rhetorical, formulaic, or supernatural character designed to bolster the Chosen One's claims to prophethood in the face of sceptical or prejudiced critics. The lapse of time before the first written sources is considerable. The first biography we have is by Ibn Ishaq who died in 767 CE, 135 years after the death of Muhammad. The version which has come down to us was extracted from a much longer work – probably a 'world history' – by Ibn Hisham (d. 833); other early biographers include al-Waqidi (d. 823) and Ibn Sa'd (d. 845). The annalist Tabari (d. 923) relates material – including the famous 'Satanic Verses' episode – not found in other sources.

The century or more of oral transmission between the life and death of Muhammad and the first biographies makes factual certainty impossible. What can be said with much more confidence is that the authority of the Quran and of Muhammad became of paramount importance in the disputes and debates that followed the Arab conquest of the Fertile Crescent. The material that found its way into the biographies appears to have been collected according to the same methodology that governed the hadiths or 'Traditions', the second tier, after the Quran, of the Muslim canon. The men who collected this material may have been as scrupulous in winnowing out reliable from unreliable traditions as circumstances allowed (see below). Modern critical scholarship, however, is bound to question this methodology. Generally, Muslim scholars are less critical, though not universally so.

The following account provides the barest essentials of a biography that would be elaborated over time to encompass the vast range of the exemplary anecdotes forming the raw material of Islamic law.

Muhammad was born around 570 CE in Makka, the site of an ancient sanctuary, one of several *hawtas* or shrines in the region where the warring tribesmen would suspend hostilities during the months of pilgrimage and perform various rituals. Non-Muslims believe the rituals to have included fertility cults such as rain-making which are found in numerous cultures. Muslim tradition holds that the square temple at the centre of the shrine, the Kaʿba, was built by Abraham (Ibrahim) near the place of sacrifice. In the Bible Abraham proves his devotion to God by offering to sacrifice Isaac, ancestor of the Hebrews, his son with the previously barren Sarah. In the Islamic version the would-be victim is Ishmael or Ismaʿil, Abraham's son with the bondwoman Hagar, who lived to become ancestor of the Arabs. The sacrifice is commemorated all over the Muslim world at the ʿId al Adha or Feast of Sacrifice which comes at the climax of the Hajj or Greater Pilgrimage, when hundreds of thousands of pilgrims flock to the sanctuary to perform the reformed or de-paganized rituals instituted by the Prophet during the final year of his life. In the traditional Muslim view, the paganism prevailing in Makka at the time of the Prophet's birth was not some 'primal' religion evolving towards monotheism, but a manifestation of religious decadence. It was a falling off or backsliding from the original 'Islam' or monotheism of Adam, Abraham, Moses, and other prophets and patriarchs.

Muhammad's tribe, the Quraish, had for several generations been guardians of the sanctuary. Makka was situated near, but not directly on, the overland trade routes linking the Mediterranean with southern Arabia and the Indian Ocean. The caravans that stopped there were making a detour because of the city's holiness. Quraishi monopoly of the shrine was institutionalized through a religious association called the Hums, the 'People of the Shrine', who distinguished themselves from the surrounding bedouin by wearing special clothes. They never left the shrine, refusing to participate in those rituals that took place outside the sacred (*haram*) area. These latter rites included the Standing at 'Arafat and the invocation of the thunder god at Muzdalifa, later incorporated by Muhammad into the Hajj ceremonies. The pilgrimage brought a measure of prosperity to the Quraish in addition to the regular products they traded in, leather and raisins. Muhammad's grandfather achieved prestige and renown as provider of food and water for the pilgrims and was responsible for re-digging the famous well of Zamzam – associated in Islamic tradition with Hagar. Orphaned at about 6, Muhammad was brought up by his grandfather and later by

Revelation described

'By the Star when it plunges,
Your comrade is not astray, neither errs,
nor speaks he out of caprice.
This is nought but a revelation revealed
taught him by one terrible in power,
very strong; he stood poised,
being on the higher horizon,
then drew near and suspended hung,
two bows' length away, or nearer,
then revealed to his servant that he revealed.
Indeed he saw him another time
by the Lote-Tree of the Boundary
nigh which is the Garden of the Refuge,
when there covered the Lote-Tree that which covered
his eye swerved not, nor swept astray.
Indeed, he saw one of the greatest signs of his Lord.'
Quran 53: 1–18

his maternal uncle Abu Talib. As a young man he entered the service of Khadija, a wealthy widow, and made several trading journeys to Syria on her behalf. She was so impressed by him that she married him. Muhammad, who is said to have married at least nine other women, remained faithful to Khadija during her lifetime. Despite her comparatively advanced age of 40, she is supposed to have born him seven children (including three sons who died in infancy).

At the age of about 40 Muhammad began undertaking regular retreats to a cave near Mt. Hira outside Makka. Scholars are divided as to whether the religious practices he adopted, including an annual retreat or *tahannuth* during the month of Ramadan, were part of the existing pagan culture, or whether he may have adopted the pious practices of Christian anchorites he met on his travels in Syria. By general consent, however, it was after a period of meditation that he received his first revelation. The awesome nature of the experience is captured in the fifty-third sura of the Quran (1–18).

Tradition, basing itself on suras revealed during the Medinese period, would identify the 'one terrible in power' as the angel Gabriel. Two western scholars, however, Richard Bell and W. Montgomery Watt argue that in these verses Muhammad believed himself to have been in the presence of God himself, like Moses on Mt. Sinai. A third visionary experience, also alluded to in one of the Quran's Makkan suras, is said to have occurred after Khadija's death, when Muhammad was transported by night 'from the sacred shrine to the distant shrine' (17: 1*). The reference was elaborated by Muslim tradition into the famous Night Journey, when Muhammad was miraculously transported to Jerusalem on the mythical beast Buraq and thence to heaven where he was instructed by God to institute the five daily prayers governing the Muslim faith. The story is consistent with shamanic experiences in many other cultures and may have been purely visionary. A hadith attributed to Muhammad's wife 'Aisha says that his body never left its place during the night in question.

Khadija accepted Muhammad's message as did his uncle's son 'Ali. For three years, according to Ibn Ishaq, Muhammad refrained from proclaiming the message in public. In a small community such as Makka, the message could not be confined to the family circle. 'People began to accept Islam, both men and women, in large numbers until the fame of it spread throughout Makka, and it began to be talked about. Then God commanded His Apostle to declare the truth of what he had received and to make known His commands to men and call them to Him'. According to Ibn Ishaq the message of Islam did not create opposition until Muhammad spoke disparagingly of the pagan deities. Western scholars suggest that during the earliest period Muhammad himself practised some of the rituals of paganism – an interpretation contested by Muslims who insist that Muhammad would never have compromised with paganism. (The issue depends in part on the dating and interpretation of certain Quranic passages such as sura 108.)

The same issue arises in the case of the so-called Satanic Verses. According to the annalist Tabari (d. 923 CE) one of the recitations revealed at Makka contained positive references to the three Makkan goddesses al-Lat, al-Uzza, and Manat as the three 'high-flying cranes' whose intercession was to be hoped for. The Quraishi opposition was overjoyed, and everyone, Muslim and pagan, joined together in prayer at the shrine. There followed an important editorial amendment: a new verse was substituted. The three goddesses 'are nought but names yourselves have named, and your fathers; God has sent down no authority touching them' (53: 19–23). The highly controversial story (which may have been invented, and does not appear in the major hadith collections) suggests to the student of religion, if not to every believer, that an evolution may have occurred in Muhammad's perception of God – from the High God of the Arabian pantheon to the Unique God without partners, associates or 'daughters'.

The Quran only hints at the Quraishi opposition to Muhammad; the historians and annalists, writing up to three centuries afterwards,

Depicting the Prophet

In the first edition of this book, this space contained an illustration from the famous manuscript of Rashid al-Din's *Universal History* (1307) in Edinburgh University Library. The picture shows the Prophet seated in a stylized rocky landscape. The Angel Gabriel, a winged figure wearing an ornate Seljuk crown, approaches him from the left with outstretched arm and pointed forefinger. In the words of the art historian David Talbot Rice 'The spirit of introverted meditation is convincingly depicted.' Although the illuminated manuscript from Tabriz is widely regarded as a masterpiece and is often reproduced, a small number of readers found the picture blasphemous. In the words of one of them: 'There is definitely no human being that can ever depict the beauty and grandeur of his [the Prophet's] countenance.' There is no explicit ban on figurative art in the Quran, but popular Muslim tradition became strongly iconophobic and manuscripts containing Muhammad's image have often been defaced.

suggest that, in addition to his attacks on idolatry, commercial interests played their part. The opposition is said to have been led by the implacable Abu Lahab, 'father of lies'. Muhammad and his immediate family were protected by Abu Talib. But some of his poorer followers were treated extremely badly, notably Bilal, the Abyssinian slave whose powerful and sonorous voice would make him the first muezzin. Fearful for their safety and fidelity to the cause Muhammad sent some of the early converts to Abyssinia, whose Christian ruler provided protection and resisted an attempt by the Quraish to have them returned to Makka. Muhammad, his clan, and those of his followers who remained in Makka were subjected to a boycott with a view to excluding them from the city's commercial life. The boycott encountered resistance from among the pagan Quraish; but just as it looked like collapsing Muhammad's uncle Abu Talib died.

Muhammad's wife Khadija died the same year. Two of his main human supporters were removed. With Khadija, his devoted wife and confidante, he shared his troubles. Abu Talib protected him from the hostility of his tribe. Deprived of his support Muhammad was increasingly exposed to the ridicule and hostility of Abu Lahab and the Quraishi aristocracy. His followers, apart from a few prestigious converts like Abu Bakr, 'Umar ibn al- Khattab, and 'Uthman ibn al-Affan – the latter a member of the important Umayyad clan – were mostly from among the poorer and less influential elements in a society where wealth, prestige, and lineage were bound up together. Nevertheless Muhammad's own prestige and reputation as a preacher extended to neighbouring districts. Bedouins who heard him at the local fairs and markets were impressed – especially a group of visitors from Yathrib, an oasis settlement about 275 miles north-east of Makka. The settlement had been divided along tribal lines, with bitter feuding between the clans, three of which, the Banu Quraiza, the Banu Qainuqa' and the Banu Nadir, had adopted a form of Judaism (just as some Arab tribes living in and around the Syrian desert adopted versions of Christianity). A delegation invited Muhammad to Yathrib (later renamed al Madina, the City of the Prophet) to act as mediator. In the year 622 CE, about twelve years after the beginning of the Prophet's mission, the Muslims made their migration (*hijra*) to Madina. The Muslim calendar is dated from the year of the Hijra (or hegira, as it is sometimes spelt in older English texts).

The Madinese suras of the Quran provide rather more historical data about the Arabian Prophet's career than those dated from the Makkan period. There are references to his raids on the Quraishi caravans when God permits fighting in the sacred month of Rajab (2: 217); and to the major victory of Badr (624 CE) when God is described as helping the Muslims with a host of angels. (The Battle of Uhud the following year,

35

when the Muslims suffer a setback, is also alluded to (3: 122–3).) There
are allusions to Muhammad's relations with the other communities of
Madina: the Ansar or Helpers who aided the Muslim emigrants, the
Munafiqun or Hypocrites who are opportunistic in their support for the
Muslims and berated for their disloyalty; and the Jews or Sons of Israel
who are derided for their errors and evidently punished for their
treachery [33: 26].

These and numerous other allusions to events which apparently
occurred are fleshed out by hadith reports transmitted over more than
a century and included in the *sira*. The Prophet acts as peacemaker in
Madina between rival tribal factions, the Aws and Khazraj and their
Jewish allies. The Jewish tribes may have been established longer in the
oasis and owned most of the date palms. 'The prosperous farms
belonged to the Jews', says a tenth-century text, the *Kitab al-Aghani*. But
the bedouin Arabs, as is often the case, have the military power. The
Jewish tribes find themselves allied to rival Arab factions. As
peacemaker the Prophet enacts a document or collection of documents
regulating the political relationship between the Emigrants, the
Helpers, and the Jews. All disputes must be referred to 'God and
Muhammad'; the Madinese will form a single community (*umma*).
Within it, however, Jews and even pagans appear to be given religious
freedom, provided they do not side with the community's enemies.
There is no clear reference to this agreement in the Quran and it is
possible that a clause allowing religious freedom for the Jews belongs to
a different document, signed after the three main Jewish tribes were
expelled or massacred.

Muhammad's relations with the Jews of Madina are as crucial for the
interpretation of early Islam as his relations with the pagan Quraish. He
respects their monotheism and accepts a common patriarchal-spiritual
lineage from Abraham, a true *hanif* or monotheist. It seems clear,
however, that, while temporarily accepting Muhammad's political
leadership, the Jews of Madina rejected him as a prophet in their

tradition. After the victory of Badr, when Muhammad's position is greatly strengthened, his relations with them deteriorate. A market place dispute leads to the expulsion of the Banu Qainuqaʿ; two years later they are followed by the Banu Nadir, accused of plotting to murder the Prophet. The following year the men of the Banu Quraiza are massacred, and their women taken into slavery, after intriguing with the Makkans during the 'Battle of the Ditch', a siege lasting several weeks when the Quraishi cavalry are kept at bay by a series of trenches ordered by the Prophet on the advice of his Persian follower Salman al-Farsi.

The political deterioration in relations with the Jews is complemented by developments on the religious front. The Quranic 'recitation', it has been suggested, becomes 'scripturalized', treated as a Book comparable to the Jewish Torah or Christian *Injil* (Gospel). The latter is conceived as a 'holy book' as distinct from an account – or series of accounts – of a holy life. The *qibla* – direction of prayer – changes from Jerusalem to Makka. The Makkan sanctuary, and part of the Makkan pagan tradition, are reappropriated in stages and given new meanings within the monotheistic, Abrahamic paradigm. In the sixth year of the Hijra Muhammad attempts the lesser pilgrimage, or ʿUmra, leading a party of Emigrants and Helpers and some of the bedouin tribesmen. The Makkans stop them from entering the sacred area; but a truce is negotiated under which the Madinans will be able to perform the pilgrimage the following year. Muhammad benefits from the peace on his southern flank to turn his attention to the rebellious Jewish tribes at the oases of Khaibar and Fadak, suspected of being in league with the Makkans. Under the terms of surrender the Jews continue to work their plantations, giving half their produce to the Muslims. After his return the Makkans honour the agreement, and Muhammad is able to lead a band of Muslims to perform the ʿUmra. However, the following year (628 CE) the truce breaks down and in January 630 he returns to the sacred city in strength. Taken by surprise, the Makkans offer no resistance. Their leader, Abu Sufyan, has been captured by the Muslims, and decides to save himself by submission to Islam.

Idolaters attacked

'. . . when the sacred months are drawn away
slay the idolaters wherever you find them,
and take them, and confine them and lie in wait
for them at every place of ambush. But if they
repent, and perform the prayer, and pay the alms, then let them
go their way;
God is all-forgiving, all-compassionate.'

(Quran 9: 5)

After circumambulating the Ka´ba and touching the Black Stone with his stick, Muhammad enters the temple and smashes the 360 idols therein, sparing only two icons of Jesus and Mary. (One traditionist, al-Azraqi, states he destroyed them miraculously, merely pointing his stick at them.) Other idols in the vicinity are destroyed, including that of the female deities al-Uzza, Manat, and al-Lat. The Prophet remains in the area of Makka and defeats a hostile bedouin confederation before making a second ´Umra to the shrine. An expedition launched to the north engages a Byzantine army at Tabuk near present-day Aqaba. The Muslim Umma is now the greatest force in the Arabian peninsula. During the year 630 CE – the Year of Delegations – most of the tribes submit; the remaining pagans are allowed the four trucial months in which to make up their minds. After that they may be killed with impunity.

The Muslim Umma has in effect become an ideological state or polity. Previously Muhammad had signed treaties with non-believers and even shared the booty of his campaigns with them. Now submission to Islam becomes the criterion of membership. In the last year of his life, 632 CE, Muhammad makes what becomes known as the Pilgrimage of Farewell. Pagans are excluded, and the rites of Hajj and ´Umra, originally two separate pagan festivals falling in spring and autumn, are compounded. The intercalary month by which the Arabs adjusted the lunar months to the solar year is abolished, severing the connection between the religious rituals and the seasons. Henceforth the pilgrimage and the Feast of Sacrifice, the central events of the Islamic calendar, will regress through the seasons, forming a complete cycle approximately every thirty-three years. Muhammad returns to Madina. Here he falls ill, and unexpectedly dies in the arms of the 18-year-old 'Aisha. God's revelations cease.

Hadith 'Traditions'

Often translated as 'Traditions' the hadiths are really discrete anecdotes about the Prophet's sayings and actions, originally passed down orally

Tolerance exemplified

'Two persons, a Muslim and a Jew, quarrelled. The Muslim said, "By Him Who gave Muhammad superiority over all the people!" The Jew said, "By Him Who gave Moses superiority over all the people!" At that the Muslim raised his hand and slapped the Jew on the face. The Jew went to the Prophet and informed him of what had happened between him and the Muslim. The Prophet sent for the Muslim and asked him about it. The Muslim informed him of the event. The Prophet said, "Do not give me superiority over Moses, for on the Day of Resurrection all the people will fall unconscious and I will be one of them, but I will be the first to gain consciousness, and will see Moses standing and holding the side of the Throne [of Allah]. I will not know whether [Moses] has also fallen unconscious and got up before me, or Allah has exempted him from that stroke."'

Bukhari, bk. 41 3: 593

and later turned into written texts. The Prophet's biography – as already stated – was constructed using the same methodology as the hadiths, with the biographers scrupulously retaining different versions of the same events and citing their sources. At first glance, the method has a transparency that is lacking in the formation of other scriptures, including the Gospels. Rather than wielding their editorial scalpels, crafting a single consistent narrative out of the oral materials available to them, the hadith collectors sifted every anecdote, report, and story according to a very different criterion. What mattered was not so much the plausibility or coherence of the story but the reliability of the sources.

The hadith collectors were aware from the first that spurious stories about the Prophet were circulating – often to support rival positions in the disputes and struggles for power that followed Muhammad's death. There is a hadith, which may or may not be authentic, according to which the Prophet is related to have said: 'He who deliberately tells lies about me will have to seek for himself a place in Hell.' Aware of the pitfalls, the hadith transmitters went to great lengths to establish the reliability of the transmitters, thoroughly investigating their characters. They developed a 'science of men' in which only the most honourable and trustworthy individuals came to be considered appropriate vehicles for the sacred task of reporting the Prophet's sayings and deeds. Hadiths were graded into varying degrees of reliability: 'sound' (*sahih*), 'good' (*hasan*), or 'weak' (*da'if*). Six collections came to acquire canonical status with two of these – the *sahihain* or 'two sound ones' of al-Bukhari (d. 870) and Muslim ibn al-Hajjaj (d. 875) – considered as second in importance only to the Quran.

Despite the efforts of the scholars the volume of hadiths continued to swell and modern critics, both Muslim and non-Muslim, have come to doubt whether the methodology was really reliable, given the long period of oral transmission before hadiths came to be written down. In India the modernist scholar Sayyid Ahmad Khan (d. 1898) began to

Birth control

'We took some women captives, and when we had sex with them we practised withdrawal (*coitus interruptus:* Arab. ʿazl) so as not to have children with them. We asked the Messenger of God about this and he said "Is that what you did?" Then he repeated three times: "There is not a soul who is to be born for the day of resurrection, but that he will be born." '

Al-Bukhari, ed. Krehl & Juynboll, *kitab al-jamʿi al-sahih* (Leiden 1868–1908), vol iii. 448, cited in John Alden Williams (ed.) *Islam* (London, 1961), 86. I have slightly modernized this translation.

question the authenticity of hadith in the nineteenth century; his associate Chirag ʿAli (d. 1898) took the view that the 'vast flood of traditions soon formed a chaotic sea. Truth and error, fact and fable, mingled together in an indistinguishable confusion'. In the West scholars such as Ignaz Goldziher and Joseph Schacht argued that the *isnads* – the chains of transmitters – had a tendency to 'grow backwards': that is to say anecdotes or reports originating at a later date with a Companion or Successor *after* the Arab conquest of the Fertile Crescent were given *isnads* tracing them back to the Prophet in order to endow them with an authority they would otherwise have lacked. In the same vein the sections containing the content of some hadiths (known as the *matn*) were identified as anachronistic: Schacht in particular argued that many fail to appear in the course of legal discussions at a time when reference to them would have been imperative.

Nowadays conservative Muslims have tended to ignore these criticisms, or to regard them as typically 'Western' attacks on Islam fuelled by religious or cultural animosity. Earlier generations were a good deal more sceptical about the character and quality of the transmitters than their descendants came to be.

Authenticity of hadith

The scepticism of early commentators regarding the authenticity of the hadith literature is illustrated by a revealing story related by the traditionist 'Umar ibn Habib, who became involved in an argument at the court of the famous Caliph Harun al-Rashid (786–809) over the merits of one of the most celebrated hadith transmitters, the Companion Abu Huraira, regarded as an unimpeachable source of the Prophet's *sunna* (custom). When his antagonists began to cast doubt on Abu Huraira's reliability 'Umar could contain himself no longer – despite the fact that the all powerful Caliph supported their position. After announcing that the hadith in question was genuine, and that Abu Huraira was a trustworthy transmitter, 'Umar received an angry look from the Caliph. When summoned to the royal presence, the Caliph said to him: 'O 'Umar ibn Habib, nobody has ever confronted me with arguments refuting and rejecting my opinion as you have!' 'O Prince of the Believers', the terrified 'Umar responded, 'Verily in what you say, and in the argument you used, there lay disrespect for the Messenger of God and for what he has brought us. If his Companions are thought of as liars, the whole *shari'a* becomes null and void; the inheritance prescriptions, as well as the rulings concerning fasting, the prayer ritual, divorce and marriage, all these ordinances will then be abolished and will no longer be accepted.' The Caliph lapsed into silence. Then he said: 'You have given me new insights. May God grant you a long life, 'Umar ibn Habib.' And he ordered that the scholar be given 10,000 dirhams.

Adapted from G. H. A. Juynboll, *Muslim Tradition* (Cambridge University Press, 1983), 197–8.

The Elaboration of Muhammad's Image

Authentic or otherwise, the hadiths became the vehicle by which the Prophet's example became the model of human behaviour for countless numbers of Muslims over the centuries. *Imitatio Christi* meant imitating Christ's suffering and adopting, ideally, his gospel of love. There are no detailed prescriptions in the New Testament about how Jesus dressed, ate, walked, cleaned his teeth, or generally comported himself, although it may be true that a composite image of his *appearance* eventually transmits itself through Christian iconography, as does that

Muhammad's appearance

'Muhammad was middle-sized, did not have lank or crisp hair, was not fat, had a white, circular face, wide black eyes and long eyelashes. When he walked, he walked as though he went down a declivity. He had the 'seal of prophecy' [a dark mole or fleshy protruberance the size of a pigeon's egg] between his shoulder blades . . . He was bulky. His face shone like the moon in the night of full moon. He was taller than middling stature, yet shorter than conspicuous tallness. He had thick curly hair. The plaits of his hair were parted . . . Muhammad had a wide forehead and fine, long, arched eyebrows which did not meet. Between his eyebrows there was a vein which distended when he was angry. The upper part of his nose was hooked; he was thick bearded, had smooth cheeks, a strong mouth and his teeth were set apart. He had thin hair on his chest. His neck was like the neck of an ivory statue, with the purity of silver. Muhammad was proportionate, stout, firm-gripped, even of belly and chest, broad-chested, and broad-shouldered.'

Annemarie Schimmel, *And Muhammad is His Messenger* (Chapel Hill: University of North Carolina Press, 1985), 34.

of the Buddha and numerous Hindu deities. *Imitatio Muhammadi* meant following the Prophet's example in every aspect of life, from ethical conduct to diet. In Islam two- or three-dimensional representations of created beings were generally forbidden (lest the artist be seen to appropriate God's creative power) and even those traditions that allowed representation in later times usually depicted the Prophet as faceless or veiled, so holy was his presence. Yet his model – idealized, no doubt, and infused with the values and aspirations of later generations – was disseminated, both orally and through the hadith literature, to become a cultural and religious icon as powerful as Christ or the Buddha, the image of *al-insan al-kamil*, the perfect or complete human being in both his worldly and spiritual aspects.

The image of the Prophet, literary rather than visual, radiates throughout the Muslim world. Perhaps the very restriction on pictorial representation aids cultural diffusion, allowing peoples of different races and ethnicities to internalize its essential features – courage, calm, compassion, *gravitas*, and holiness. Muhammad claimed no superhuman qualities for himself. 'Say . . . "I am only a warner, and a herald of glad tidings to people who believe"' [7: 188]. Yet the *siras* are full of supernatural episodes which would later acquire elaborate legendary accretions. The story emanating from the opening of sura 94, 'Have we not opened up thy heart and lifted from thee the burden that had weighed so heavily on thy back?', is elaborated in hadiths about angelic visitors who take him to a mountain top, open his breast, and remove the heart, which is cleansed with snow and replaced after a 'black speck, filled with blood', representing 'Satan's part in him', has been removed. Thus guaranteed, the Prophet's sinlessness makes him the immaculate source of emulation for later generations. However, as Annemarie Schimmel points out, there was no official doctrine concerning the prophet's sinlessness in the earliest days of Islam, and the first generation of historians and commentators were less concerned than their successors would be with exonerating him from taking any part in the pagan rituals of Makka before Allah guided him to the worship of the one true God.

A similar edifice of legend and poetic imagery accrues around the opening of the fifty-fourth sura 'The last hour draws near and the moon is split asunder!'* While modernists and some other commentators sought to demythologize the phrase by pointing to its eschatological context – along with other marvels as the Day of Judgement approaches, the moon will split – most of the early commentators saw it as a reference to an actual event described in several hadiths attributed to the Prophet's companions, according to which the moon appeared one night as if split into separate parts. In popular tradition as in mystical poetry the 'splitting of the moon' becomes one of

Muhammad as model

'Know that the key to happiness is to follow the Sunna and to imitate the Messenger of God in all his coming and going, his movements and rest, in his way of eating, his attitude, his sleep and his talk. I do not mean this in regard to religious observance, for there is no reason to neglect the traditions which were concerned with this aspect. I rather mean all the problems of custom and usage, for only by following them unrestricted succession is possible. God has said: "Say: If you love God, follow me, and God will love you" (sura 3: 29), and He has said: "What the messenger has brought – accept it, and what he has prohibited – refrain from it!" (sura 59: 7). That means, you have to sit while putting on trousers, and to stand when winding a turban, and to begin with the right foot when putting on shoes."'

Ghazali, *Ihya 'ulum al Din* 2: 300–44, tr. Leo Zolondek (Leiden: Brill, 1963), cited by Schimmel, 31.

Muhammad's greatest miracles, celebrated in Sindhi, Punjabi, Swahili, and other Muslim languages. In other miracle stories the Prophet emulates the Quranic Jesus by breathing life into a bird of stone, produces rain after drought or water from between his fingers, and causes a solitary barren sheep to provide enough milk for his thirsty companions and himself. Another food miracle in which 1,000 people are fed from a single sheep recalls the Feeding of the Five Thousand in the New Testament. Camels and wild beasts prostrate themselves before Muhammad, knowing him to be a messenger sent by God, along with inanimate things such as rocks and stones and trees. The great Persian poet Jami proclaims:

> A little stone, smaller than a rosary's bead
> Recited in his hand with eloquent words the praise of God,
> And those eloquent ones whose hearts were black as stone,
> Were unison in silence.

Those to whom the Prophet appears in dreams cannot be deceived, for God will not permit Satan to take his form, and on waking their chambers will be filled with the pleasant scent of musk. To allow for imposture – a false vision of the Prophet – would undermine the unity of Islam by inviting accusations and counter-accusations of fraud. By the same logic the Muslim mystic is denied direct access to divine revelation, for Muhammad is the 'seal' of the prophets, the final revelator sent by God to humankind. Visions of the Prophet are not just *ipso facto* authentic – they guarantee that the mystics and visionaries to whom they are vouchsafed remain within the Islamic fold. Where a mystic or holy man is claimed to have been the recipient of direct revelation – as in the case of Mirza Ghulam Ahmad, founder of the proselytizing Ahmadiyya sect – controversy and accusations of heresy will dog his followers.

Muhammad's role as a source of emulation, however, is far from being confined to mystics and visionaries. The physical details of his life – the

46

Muhammad's inaccessibility

'Our culture can no longer move in this universe it calls magical, superstitious, unreal, irrational, imaginary, marvellous, fabulous and legendary. All this vocabulary conveys difference, rejection, distance and disqualification rather than integration into a comprehensive realm of intelligibility capable of accommodating all the facts and phenomena presented for analysis. The religious experience and historical activity of Muhammad emerges and unfurls precisely in this semiological universe we no longer understand.'

Mohamed Arkoun, *Rethinking Islam: Common Questions, Uncommon Answers*, tr. and ed. Robert D. Lee (Boulder, Colorado: Westview Press (1994)), 43.

cut of his beard, the clothes he wore, the food he liked, as reported in the hadith literature – came to be seen as models of human comportment and human behaviour. Some people avoided certain foods such as garlic, mangoes, and melons, because he was reported to have disliked them, or because there was no record that he had eaten them. Honey and mutton were cherished because he cherished them; dogs were considered unclean because – according to a well-known hadith – 'the angels do not enter a house in which there is a dog or statues'; but cats were approved of because – as he Is related to have said – they are among the animals that grace human dwellings. The medieval mind saw in his every activity the perfection of conduct, his every opinion a direct guidance from God.

Muhammad, like Jesus and the founders of other world religions, is a bridge between myth and history, the realms, respectively, of divine and human action. He inhabits a world where historical activity is surrounded by supernatural forces, where the numinous constantly interpenetrates the dull sublunary world of common sense. To grasp this world in its fullness must lie beyond our capacities as moderns. Scholars of varying disciplines can only hope to analyse fragments of the vast cultural imaginative and historical residue left from the two decades when God addressed humanity – as Muslims see it – through the words of the last of his prophets.

Chapter 3
Divine Unicity

Tawhid: Introduction

If there is a single word that can be taken to represent the primary
impulse of Islam, be it theological, political, or sociological, it is *tawhid* –
making one, unicity. Although the word does not occur in the Quran,
the concept it articulates is implicit in the credal formula *there is no god
but God* and there are references to the God who is without partners or
associates throughout the holy text. The absolute insistence that it is
Unicity above all that defines divinity appears in striking, if ironic,
contrast with the disunity observable in the Muslim world. It is as if the
aspiration to realize divine unicity in terms of the social and political
order is forever destined to wreck itself on the shores of human
perversity.

God's unity

*'Say: He is God, One,
God, the Everlasting Refuge,
who has not begotten, and has not been begotten,
and equal to Him there is not any one.'*
[Quran sura 112]

---

4. The Dome of the Rock and al-Aqsa Mosque in Jerusalem. A masterpiece in the Byzantine style, the Dome of the Rock proclaimed the unity of God while celebrating the triumph of Islam over Christianity.

The overwhelming stress on God's uniqueness reflects the polemical context in which early Islam was forged. *Tawhid* simultaneously challenges Arabian paganism, Zoroastrian dualism, and the Christian doctrine of divine incarnation in language that recalls, and deliberately harks back to, the uncompromising monotheism of the Hebrew prophets. The first great building constructed by the conquering Arabs in Palestine – the Dome of the Rock on Jerusalem's Holy Mount – occupies the site of the Jewish Temple on ground where Jewish tradition supposes that Abraham sacrificed his son, and where in later times the Ark of the Covenant came to rest. The exquisite octagonal building, with its marble cladding and golden dome, is decorated with Quranic inscriptions proclaiming God's unity and Muhammad's prophethood. The same inscriptions appear on the coinage minted by its builder, the Caliph 'Abd al-Malik (r. 685–705). The new shrine is close to the spot from where Muhammad is supposed to have ascended to heaven on his Night Journey, when, according to Islamic tradition, he was received by Abraham and Moses, and taught the duties of prayer. The shrine is dedicated to the religion of Abraham. It replaces and supersedes the Temple of Solomon and mounts a direct challenge to Christianity, the imperial faith of Byzantium.

The First Sectarian Divisions

Unity of empire is the reflection of divine unity, a unity compromised by the errors of the Jews and the false doctrines (divine incarnation, vicarious atonement for sin) of the Christians. Yet from the very first, according to Islam's sacred narrative, that terrestrial unity is compromised by the Muslims themselves. Muhammad's death in 632 CE creates a crisis of authority that has never been resolved. Abu Bakr, his close companion and father of his favourite wife ʿAisha, is elected leader in Medina, following Arab tribal custom. The claims of ʿAli,

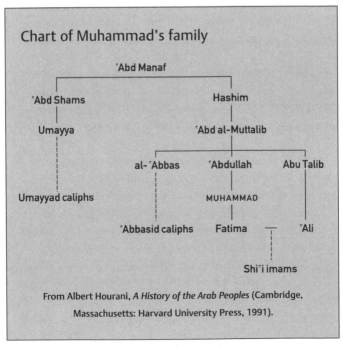

Chart of Muhammad's family

From Albert Hourani, *A History of the Arab Peoples* (Cambridge, Massachusetts: Harvard University Press, 1991).

Muhammad's cousin and son-in-law, his closest male relative, are bypassed on this and two subsequent occasions. Only after the death of 'Uthman does 'Ali come into what his Partisans (Arab. Shi'a) regard as his lawful inheritance. But by now it is too late. 'Ali's leadership is contested, and he fails to impose his authority over the whole community. The garrisons based in Iraq support him; the troops based in Syria under the command of Mu'awiya resist, and an attempted compromise, promoted by 'Ali in the interests of unity, collapses in acrimony. Some of 'Ali's supporters are so disillusioned that they leave his camp, becoming known as 'Seceders' (*khawarij* – lit. 'those who go out'), a name that becomes attached to the first separate sect in Islam. One of them, Ibn Muljam, assassinates 'Ali – and so the tragic history of Shi'ism begins. 'Ali's eldest son Hasan compromises with Mu'awiya, living quietly in Medina. It is his younger brother Hussein who, on Mu'awiya's death in 680, raises the standard of revolt, and dies on the field of Karbala on the banks of the Euphrates, cut down by the troops of Mu'awiya's son Yazid.

These early disputes are largely, if not exclusively, concerned with power. Who has the right to leadership, by what authority? But they also acquire a distinctively religious colouring as the issue of leadership and authority is perceived as necessary to salvation.

The Imams or leaders in the line of 'Ali demonstrate not the unity of Islam, but rather its opposite. Popular support for the Shi'i cause, among those who feel that the wordly rulers of the Islamic empire have betrayed its message of unity, peace, and social justice, is never lacking. In 749 a Shi'i-inspired movement leads to the formation of a new dynasty that moves the capital from Syria to Iraq. To the disappointment of many of its supporters, however, the new ruler turns out to be a descendant not of 'Ali, but of Muhammad's uncle 'Abbas: closer to the Holy Family than the 'Umayyads, but not of the Prophet's progeny. This further betrayal inspires the Shi'i Leader of the day, the Imam Ja'far, to adopt a more quietist approach in the manner of Hasan rather than Hussein. Despite their acquiescence in *de facto* reality of non-'Alid power, Shi'i Imams remain a thorn in the side of the new 'Abbasid caliphs. In the sacred history of Shi'ism, each Imam in turn is secretly murdered – usually by poisoning. Eventually the Twelfth Imam, Muhammad al Muntazar – the Awaited One – disappears altogether. He will return at the end of time as the Messiah (al-Mahdi) to bring peace, justice, and unity to a world torn by corruption, division, and strife. It is a convenient solution to the problem of an underground, but divinely guided, leader: given the doubts that must always surround a succession in these circumstances, it may be easier to build a consensus around an absent Imam than one who is living underground.

Thereafter Shi'ism will oscillate between quietism and activism. Just as the Seceders eventually establish separatist communities on the fringes of the Islamic world, in the Tunisian desert, Oman, and Zanzibar, where they are known as Ibadis, so various factions of Shi'a create separate polities outside the metropolitan areas: in Tabaristan, Yemen, North Africa, and the Gulf. At times leaders of the Shi'a counsel caution. A doctrine known as *taqiya* – dissimulation – allows the believers to conceal their true allegiance to the Imams if they fear for their safety: the cruel injustices inflicted on the Family of Muhammad and their followers will have to wait for the return of the Hidden Imam before being rectified. But the eschatological expectations surrounding the Hidden Imam can also inspire and legitimize revolts, some of which lead to permanent changes of government. The example of the Prophet's grandsons Hasan and Hussein, the quietist and the activist, can be invoked to justify either course.

Other Branches of Shi'ism

The followers of the Twelfth Imam, who now number some 80 million in Iran (where Shi'ism is the state religion), Iraq, Afghanistan, Pakistan, Azerbaijan, Syria, Lebanon, Turkey, and the Gulf, are usually known as Imamis or Ithna'asharis ('Twelvers'). A minority sect of the Shi'a, however, claims allegiance to Isma'il, eldest son of the Imam Ja'far whom Twelvers believe to have predeceased his father or to have been passed over. Sometimes known as Seveners, they are generally called Isma'ilis. During the tenth century CE these Isma'ilis were at the forefront of several revolts inspired by eschatological expectations. In 909 a leader claiming descent from Isma'il proclaims himself the Mahdi and creates a state in North Africa. His son's general successfully invades Egypt, founding a caliphate there (which becomes known as the Fatimid caliphate, after the Prophet's daughter). The Fatimids reign for more than two centuries, until 1171, when they are replaced by the Sunni hero Salah al-Din al-Ayyubi – known to the West as Saladin – liberator of Jerusalem from the Crusaders. Though Egypt is brought back into the

The passion plays

'Elsewhere, in towns but above all in villages, the ta'ziya is held. This religious theatre is so extraordinary, so popular and so spontaneous. It gathers all around a scene improvised in the open air (or in the husseiniya). The spectators and actors are interchangeable: everyone knows Yazid, 'Ali, Akbar, Zeinab and Hazrat 'Abbas . . . they are the ones in the village who can read and have decked themselves out for the occasion in the costumes of the drama. They have their script in their hands and the director asks them to read their part, handing each the microphone in his turn. There is magic, with horses stampeded through the midst of it all, firecrackers that explode during the battle, the hand of 'Abbas that flies through the air before managing to get water from the Euphrates (symbolised by a bathtub) to assuage the thirst of Hussein's companions. There is blood, the clashing of sabres, whirled round over heads, the beating of drums and the sound of death cries.'

Yann Richard, Shi'ite Islam (Oxford: Blackwell, 1995), 99.

Sunni fold, the Isma'ili communities survive in mountain strongholds in Syria, Persia and Yemen. Their descendants include two prosperous modern groups from India – the Musta'lian Bohras and the Nizari Isma'ilis. The latter are the only group of Shi'a who still claim allegiance to a living Imam – the Imam in the line of the Fatimid Caliph al-Musta'li having also 'disappeared'. The Nizaris, now widely distributed in India, Pakistan, East Africa, Europe, and North America as well as western China and central Asia, believe that their current Imam, known by his Persian title of Aga Khan, is the forty-ninth Imam in direct line of descent from 'Ali. Another important branch of the Shi'a allegiance are the Zaidis of Yemen, numbering some three millions, who recognize Zaid ibn 'Ali (grandson of Hussein who died at Karbala), instead of his brother Muhammad al-Baqir as fifth imam. Other surviving off-shoots of the Shi'a include the Druzes of Lebanon, who describe themselves as Unitarians (*muwahiddun*), laying particular stress on *tawhid* as taught by sixth Fatimid Caliph al-Hakim bi Amr Allah (996–1021), the 'Alawis of Syria (also known as Nusairis), and the Babis of Iran, a nineteenth-century messianic movement which gave birth to the separate religion of Bahaism.

Issues of leadership rather than doctrine were originally at the heart of the dispute between the Shi'a and what become the Sunni majority. But over time disputes about politics acquire a theological dimension. The 'massacre' of Karbala, a fight between rival clans that only lasts a day and results in a few dozen dead, becomes the defining myth of Shi'ism, an emblem of suffering and martyrdom. Re-enacted on the anniversary in every Shi'i village with processions of bloody flagellants who punish themselves for the betraying of the Prophet's grandson, it does for Shi'ism what Christ's Passion does for Catholicism: it reconciles the believer to the world's injustices, while offering the promise of redemption. The Imams acquire a supernatural dimension. They are the sources of esoteric scriptural knowledge, bearers of the Divine Light of Truth since the creation, who alone can understand and decode the meanings of scripture. In the Twelver and Musta'lian Isma'ili traditions, the absent Imam's authority is exercised on his behalf by religious professionals or deputies. Among the Twelvers this delegation has led to the elaboration of a hierarchy comparable to the Christian priesthood, without possessing its formal sacerdotal powers.

The Shi'i Imamate

'The Imamate is to some extent the consequence and the application of the principle of justice to the guidance of humankind. God, who created men, could not let them go to their perdition. That is why He sent them the prophets, the last of whom was Muhammad, to guide them along the path of justice and truth. But after the death of the last prophet it was unthinkable that God in His wisdom should leave men to their own devices without there being, in every era, a spiritual guarantor, proof of the truth of the revelation, to direct the community: this is the Imam, the "Guide". As he plays a fundamental role in the relations between God and men, the Imam cannot be chosen by fallible men and left to the vicissitudes of history: he must fulfil certain conditions of principle, be perfectly learned in religious matters, be absolutely just and equitable, be perfect, free from any fault, be the most perfect man of his time; it is inconceivable that someone more perfect should obey another less perfect ... The Imam is designated by a supernatural investiture (*nass*) coming from God by the intermediary of the Prophet or the Imam who has preceded him: he receives his authority from on high. Thus the infallible Imam links the human community with the invisible world.'

Richard, *Shi'ite Islam*, 6.

Tawhid in Early Islamic Thought

For the Sunni *'ulama* the doctrine of God's unicity has ramifications primarily in terms of law. It is not for humans to speculate on the nature of God. Rather, it is their duty to obey his commands. In its most extreme formulation, human laws have no authority underpinning them. Only the laws of God, embodied in the Shari'a, demand obedience. Such insistence on giving priority to God's commands as distinct from his Nature or Being, however, was never enough to satisfy speculative minds or the mystical orientation of those who sought to penetrate the inner experience of the divine. Early theological debates centred on such questions as the status of sinners, free will and predestination, God's justice, and the anthropomorphic attributions of God in the Quran.

The issue of sinners involved the fundamental question 'Who is a Muslim?' The first radical splinter group, the Khawarij or Seceders, believed that serious sinners such as adulterers had *ipso facto* excluded themselves from the community and could no longer be considered Muslims. At the other end of the spectrum a group known as the Murjia, whose best-known spokesman was Abu Hanifa, founder of the most liberal of the schools of law, argued that anyone making the profession of faith (the Shahada) was a Muslim: their sins would be judged by God. This doctrine encouraged conversions to Islam among peoples on the fringes, such as central Asian nomads; but it made the need for legal enforcement less compelling: if everything is to be left to the judgement of God, what is the point of implementing the law? To this the learned men among the People of the Sunna or 'traditionalists' had their answer. The sinner can still be a Muslim, but there are different degrees of faith and a person's standing in the community (and, by extension, the desirable aim of creating a virtuous society) is determined by good works.

Arguments over sin inevitably lead to the broader question of free will

Divine Unity

and predestination. Does God know in advance who is going to sin? Is he bound by his own rules of justice? Must he reward virtue and punish wrongdoing? Or does this impinge on his freedom of action, his omnipotence? The argument about God's justice was deeply bound up with the question of God's unicity and with the status of revelation itself. In one of the earliest passages of the Quran revealed to the Prophet in Makka 'God' – speaking through Muhammad – curses Muhammad's chief Quraishi opponent, Abu Lahab, for his persistent opposition, and predicts for him a roasting in hell (Quran 111). If Abu Lahab was a free agent, able to choose between acceptance and rejection of God's message, it followed that the Quran must already have been 'created' when this message was 'sent down'. To suggest otherwise would be to argue that God had already predetermined Abu Lahab's fate, depriving him of freedom of action. The doctrine of the Created Quran, however, ran into powerful opposition from the traditionalists, who saw it as derogating from the idea of the Quran as God's speech. The group of theologians known as the Mu'tazila who espoused the doctrine of the Created Quran adopted a rationalist style of argumentation influenced by the Greek philosophers. For them divine unicity was compromised by the doctrine of an Uncreated Quran. The argument was further complicated by the presence in the Quran of certain anthropomorphic expressions, such as God's face, hands, eyes, throne, and so forth. For the Mu'tazila who were also known as the People of Unity and Justice, literal interpretations of such expressions smacked of *shirk* – 'associationism' or 'idolatry': the association of lesser, i.e. created, beings with God, detracting from his transcendental 'otherness'. Expressions such as God's 'face' must be understood as referring to his essence, his 'eyes' as his capacity to see.

The rationalist tendency held sway at the 'Abbasid court under the Caliph Al-Mamun (813–33) who imposed an inquisition-type system, the *mihna*, according to which government officials were obliged to declare their allegiance to the doctrine of the Created Quran. One who refused to do so, despite imprisonment and torture, was Ahmad Ibn Hanbal, the traditionist, who subsequently became a hero for the anti-Mu'tazili People of the Sunna and Community.

In 849, under one of al-Mamun's successors, the policy was reversed. Theological underpinning for a compromise between the rationalists and traditionalists was supplied by a former Mu'tazili, Abu'l Hasan al-Ash'ari (d. 935). Ash'ari and his followers insisted that the Quran was uncreated and that God has foreknowledge of human action, as described in the Quran. He argued, however, that God's omniscience and human responsibility could be accommodated by a doctrine of 'acquisition' whereby God creates the power for people to 'acquire' actions created by him at the instant of action. The Ash'aris were satisfied that their doctrine preserved God's monopoly of creation, hence his unicity. Ash'ari denounced the Mu'tazili attempts to allegorize or de-anthropomorphize the Quranic deity's attributes by stating that they existed in addition to his essence. If the divine will were perceived as one with the divine essence (as the Mu'tazila argued), then divine unicity was indeed compromised, for God's freedom of choice was called into question. Ultimately, for the Ash'aris, God is inaccessible to human reason. God makes himself known only through revelation, and the terms in which he chooses to reveal himself (including his throne, his hands etc.) must be accepted 'without asking how' – *bila kaif*. This phrase, a key term in Ash'ari theology, 'leaves to God the understanding of his own mystery'.

The Sunni Consensus

For centuries Ash'ari theology held sway over what became known as Sunni Islam. With the débâcle of the *mihna* the attempted fusion of religious and political authority in the caliphate was seen to have failed. Religious leadership remained for the most part in the hands of the *'ulama* – a class of religious scholars whose authority was based on their knowledge of scripture, but not on hierocratic or spiritual power. There is no clear 'pecking order' among the Sunni *'ulama*: just as among

American Protestants virtually anyone with a basic theological training can become a preacher, so amongst Sunnis 'any qualified [Islamic] lawyer can declare whether something is against Islamic law, so there can be as many versions of "orthopraxy" as there are jurists'. Generally decentralized religious authority (as in American Protestantism) tends towards conservatism. Without a cult of divinely inspired leadership the text becomes paramount, and even if the text itself is deemed to be divine, interpretation is most likely to proceed in the safety of well-worn grooves.

Theosophical Speculations

The Sunni consensus may have opted for the safety of focusing on God's commands rather than indulging in speculation about his nature; but after their first encounters with Helleno-Christian thought some Muslim intellectuals refused to be put off by *bila kaif*, going to considerable lengths to reconcile the Quranic deity with the God of the philosophers. As they developed an increasingly sophisticated discourse, the Islamic philosophers gradually moved away from the 'Quranic God who creates, acts in time, guides mankind and who can in some way, albeit indirectly, be known' towards 'an utterly remote, unknowable God who does not even create'. The systems they constructed vary as do their terminologies. Common to most of them, however, are ideas of emanation derived from Neoplatonism and in particular the philosopher Plotinus (c. 204–70 CE), who defined God, 'the One [who] is in truth beyond all statement and affirmation', in negative as well as positive terms. This *via negativa* is consistent with the Islamic credal formula, which begins with the negative '*There is no god . . .*'; God's positive dimension could still be approached through his 'great names' of which there are ninety-nine in the Quran. Creation comes not directly from God but through a series of emanations – the First Intellect, the Second Intellect, the First Heaven and so forth – that correspond to the various medieval cosmologies. God himself remains intact, uninfringed, unexplained, and inexplicable. The Persian philosopher Ibn Sina

(Avicenna) (979–1037), arguing that God has knowledge of generalities but not particulars, emphasizes the gulf between the philosophical god and the God of Quranic theology, to the annoyance of the conservatives.

However, speculation about God was allowed to flourish under the patronage of the Isma'ili Imams who elevated reason or intellect to the highest level beneath the unknown and unknowable deity. This God is not in himself the cause of things: his being is beyond the whole chain of existence, of cause and effect. Isma'ili cosmologies varied in their details, but they shared common features, including an emphasis on a Transcendent Deity, unknown and unknowable; a system of emanations linked into the Isma'ili hierarchy with the Imam at its head and a cyclical view of history according to which each era has its prophet and his 'silent' companion who knows the inner meanings of the scriptures. Unabashed élitists, the Isma'ilis developed their system against a background of differential hermeneutics whereby the literal or exoteric meanings of the Quran were accessible to the many, while the 'inner' or esoteric meanings were known only to the few. For example Isma'ili writers would interpret the Quranic descriptions of heaven and hell as referring to states of being rather than physical places of bliss or torment. The true meaning of scripture was known to the Imam and the *da'is* or missionaries appointed by him. Though not a 'paid up member' of the Isma'ili movement, Ibn Sina may be said to have been a fellow-traveller. Likewise the great Spanish philosopher Ibn Rushd (Averroës) (1126–98) has been described as 'almost a closet Isma'ili' in his acceptance of differential hermeneutics. For Ibn Rushd, the ordinary people are required to accept the Quran in its literal or exoteric sense lest they be led into *kufr* (disbelief) whereas the philosophers have much more discretion in interpreting scriptural truth. Ibn Rushd, who in addition to being a philosopher acted as a judge charged with the implementation of the Shari'a, has been accused of 'double standards' in preaching 'one truth for the masses, and another for the elect'. A more tactful way of putting it, however, is to say that, like the Isma'ilis, 'he is a proponent of a multivocal expression of truth'. It is generally accepted that Ibn Rushd's influence was greater in the medieval West than in the Muslim world.

Sufism

It was not only the philosophers and intellectuals who rejected literalistic interpretations of scripture. The mystically inclined Sufis – named after the coarse shirts of wool (*souf*) worn by some early adepts – rejected or de-emphasized outward or formalistic forms of observance in favour of a style of pietism that sought to apprehend the reality of God's unity through direct experience. Scholars have suggested that early Sufis may have been influenced by mystical tendencies among

The Sura of Light

'God is the Light
Of the heavens and the earth
The parable of His light
Is as if there were a niche
And within it a lamp
The lamp enclosed in a glass
The glass as it were a brilliant star
Lit from a blessed tree,
An olive neither of the East nor of the West
Whose oil is well-nigh luminous
Though fire scarce touched it:
Light upon light!
God doth guide
Whom He will
To His light.'
(Quran 24: 35)

Eastern Christians, gnostics (who abounded in the ancient Near East in important intellectual centres such as Alexandria), central Asian shamans and even yogis from India. But there are many Quranic passages that lend themselves to a mystical interpretation, most famously a verse in the Sura of Light (24: 35) which dwells on the theme of divine radiance.

Among the earliest Sufi adepts was the famous Rabi'a al-Adawiya, a poet of Basra who defied convention by eschewing marriage, and would run through the streets of the city with a torch in one hand and a jug of water in the other: 'I am going to light fire in Paradise and pour water onto Hell, so that both veils may be taken away from those who journey towards God [that] they may look towards their Sustainer without any object of hope or motive of fear.' The pure, disinterested love of God, without hope of reward or fear of punishment, is the leitmotif of Sufism throughout the centuries. The Sufi adept, through spiritual disciplines such as yogic breathing while pronouncing the pronoun 'He' (*hua*) in

God's love

'The Sufis teach that the natural love of humans for each other is necessary to show one the way to the love of God. The lover who "passes away" has no carnal soul left ... the friends of God, by loving one another, bear witness to the reality of love, as do animals and the works of the Divine Artist, which manifest Universal Beauty. The lovers of God reach either unitive fusion with him (*ittihad*, a concept condemned in later Sufism) or the "station" of experiencing God's Uniqueness (*tawhid*) which means reaching him, so that he seems both to be and not to be in and through everything.'

Julian Baldick, *Mystical Islam: An Introduction to Sufism* (London: Tauris, 1989), 57.

5. Sufis performing the *dhikr* – 'remembrance' of God – near Omdurman, Sudan. Sufi rituals celebrate the divine in a purely disinterested way: the focus is on the absolute transcendence of God as distinct from His attributes, such as Mercy and Compassion.

remembrance of God, ultimately aspires to the state of *fana*, union with God. But Sufism also influences less mystically oriented souls, such as the great jurist and theologican Abu Hamid al-Ghazali (d. 1111) and Hasan al-Banna (1906–49) founder of the Muslim Brotherhood. Ghazali left his teaching post in Baghdad and spent several years as a Sufi travelling to Syria and Palestine before writing his famous *Ihya 'ulum al-din* – 'The Revitalisation of the Religious Sciences' – a book which infuses the strict orthopraxy of Sunnism with a powerful dose of mystical piety, so that every activity from defecation to prayer becomes in its own way a 'remembrance of God'. The *Ihya* was Hasan al-Banna's bedside reading. With Ghazali, as with other writers belonging to the so-called 'sober' Sufis, the law remains the frame through which mystical feeling must manifest itself. But mystical enthusiasm can also take radical antinomian forms which transgress the rules of the Shari'a and sometimes scandalize the pious.

The famous mystic al-Hallaj (857–922) described his spiritual union with

God in language ('I am the Truth') that the powers of the time saw as threatening to the authority of the caliph and the ʿulama. He was crucified and burned, his ashes thrown into the river Tigris. The official reason for his execution was his teaching that the pilgrimage to Makka could be performed spiritually while staying at home. Despite occasional persecution, 'drunken' or ecstatic Sufism persisted alongside legalistic Islam. It animates Sufi-inspired poetry with constantly recurring images of divine love, challenging the conventional religiosity of what might be called 'the ʿulama establishment'. Sufis often flirted

Beyond language

'In the name of God the Merciful the Compassionate and Him we ask for aid: Praise be to God before whose Oneness there was not a before, unless the Before were He, and after whose singleness there is not an after except that After be He. He is and there is with Him no after nor before, nor above nor below, nor far nor near, nor union nor division, nor how nor where nor when, nor times nor moment nor age, nor being nor place. And He is now as He was. He is the One without oneness, and the Single without singleness. He is not composed of names and named, for His name is He and His named is He. So there is no name other than He, nor named. And so He is the Name and the Named. He is the First without firstness, and the Last without lastness. He is the Outward without outwardness, and the Inward without inwardness. I mean that He is the very existence of the Outward and the very existence of the Inward. So that there is no first nor last, nor outward nor inward, except Him, without these becoming Him or His becoming them.'

Ibn ʿArabi, 'Whoso Knoweth Himself . . .', from the Treatise on
Being – risalat-ul-wujudiyya, tr. T. H. Weir (London: Beshara
Publications, 1976), 3.

with public obloquy and social danger, as if to prove that their love of God was wholly disinterested, uninfluenced by, indeed, contemptuous of, the social approval sought by the outwardly pious. Wine, forbidden to Muslims, becomes the emblem of divinity: homoeroticism (forbidden in theory, though not always in practice) is a recurring theme, where the divine is manifested in the beauty of beardless boys.

Sufis sometimes derided the intellectual approach to the understanding of *tawhid* adopted by Isma'ilis and other Neoplatonists, but in the writings of Ibn 'Arabi (1165–1240) whom many regard as the greatest of Sufi masters, the two approaches are fused. Ibn 'Arabi is sometimes accused of pantheism for his statement that 'nothing exists except Allah'. However, his system makes a categorical distinction between God's essence, which cannot be known or experienced by the mystic, and the level of unicity to which the mystic can aspire through the revelation of God's names. The 'inner reality' of Muhammad is identified with the First or Universal Intellect of the Neoplatonic system, deemed to have existed from all eternity, and with the Perfect Man of Sufi terminology – the microcosmic being through whom God contemplates himself, as in a mirror. Ibn 'Arabi could thus be described as a 'mystical humanist' for 'in a very real way [his] man is somehow God (in a sense that he is one with God like all things) and God is simply somehow man', though God is also much more than that. Ibn 'Arabi's system has been described as the 'ultimate theological semiosis in Islamic thought: everything signifies, and everything signifies only the One Reality, God'.

Sufism and Shi'ism

The Sufi masters, renowned for their spirituality, are known as 'friends' (*walis*) of God, a term sometimes translated as 'saints', though as there is no church in Islam there are no formal processes of canonization. The intercessionary powers attributed to God's Friends endow them with the religious authority that leads to the creation of the Sufi orders (see Chapter 6). Inevitably there is considerable overlapping between the spiritual authority of the Imams and that of the Friends. Indeed, according to the Shi'i version of the declaration of faith, *There is no god but God, Muhammad is the Messenger of God, 'Ali is the Friend of God*. Just as 'Ali follows immediately after Muhammad in the chain of authorities through which some Sufi orders trace their respective rules, so the founders of Sufi orders are granted the same powers of interpretation into the esoteric meanings of scripture the Shi'a reserve for their Imams. Like the Imams, only the 'friends' are credited with fully understanding the Quran. Both Sufism and Shi'ism infuse the law with spiritual meanings; both endow their leaders with a measure of supernatural authority; both seek to establish avenues to illumination inspired by love of God rather than fear of punishment.

Shi'ism and Iran

Iran has been a Shi'i state since the sixteenth century when Shah Isma'il, founder of the Safavid dynasty (1501–1722), persuaded a group of Turcoman nomads that he was the Hidden Imam and launched a successful invasion. The Safavid rulers and their successors, the Qajars, eventually retreated from these claims, allowing a parallel system to develop in which the Shi'i *ulama* acquired a considerable degree of autonomy. Under the Safavids the synthesis of Neoplatonism and Sufi gnosis reached a further stage in the work of Mulla Sadra of Shiraz (1572–1641). Drawing on the illuminationist philosophy of al-Suhrawardi (d. 1191), Mulla Sadra believed that the divine light of knowledge flowed down through an unbroken chain from Adam, the first prophet, through the Greek philosophers (including Empedocles, Pythagoras, Socrates, Plato, Aristotle, and Plotinus), through Muhammad, the Imams and the Sufi masters, notably Ibn 'Arabi. His system admits no contradiction between free will and determinism, the God of philosophy and that of the Quran. Rational arguments are buttressed by intuitive, subjective experience in Mulla Sadra's scheme. However, scholars are far from unanimous about how successful he was in reconciling the two.

The glory of *tawhid*

'The world view of *tawhid* is backed by the force of logic, science and reason. In every particle of the universe, there are indications of the existence of a wise, omniscient God; every tree leaf is a compendium of knowledge of the solicitous Lord.

The world view of *tawhid* gives meaning, spirit and aim to life because it sets man on the course of perfection that stops at no determinate limit but leads ever onward.

The world view of *tawhid* has a magnetic attraction; it imparts joy and confidence to man; it presents sublime and sacred aims; and it leads individuals to be self-sacrificing.

The world view of *tawhid* is the only world view in which individuals' mutual commitment and responsibility find meaning, just as it is the only world view that saves man from falling into the terrible valley of belief in futility and worship of nothingness.'

Ayatullah Murtaza Mutahhari, *Fundamentals of Islamic Thought: God, Man and the Universe*, tr. R. Campbell (Berkeley, California: Mizan Press, 1985), 74.

Despite the opposition of some of the ʿulama, philosophical speculation has never been extinguished in the Shiʿi tradition. The appearance of modernist ideas involved less of a disjunction of tradition than among the Sunnis. As deputies of the Hidden Imam the mullahs exercise the right of *ijtihad* – independent interpretation of the Shariʿa – in contrast to most of their Sunni counterparts, who until recently tended to be bound by *taqlid* – 'imitation' of precedents applied by their predecessors. Mulla Sadra remains an important influence on such modern Shi'i clerical thinkers as Muhammad Hussein al-Tabataba'i and Murtaza Mutahhari, as well as on lay thinkers such as 'Ali Shariati and Seyyed Hossein Nasr.

The authority of the Shi'i clergy is reinforced by the considerable wealth they dispose of as trustees of the numerous Shi'i shrines, recipients of religious taxes such as *zakat* and *khums*, and the corporate owners of urban and agricultural estates (for example, a religious endowment administered by the clergy owns more than half of Mashhad, Iran's eastern regional capital, a city of more than one million inhabitants). Prior to 1979 they had a long history of defiance to the state. In 1890 they launched a nation-wide boycott of all tobacco goods in protest against the granting of a royal monopoly to an Englishman, forcing the Shah into a humiliating retreat. This triumph led directly to constitutional revolution in 1905-6, in which the clergy played a leading, if ambivalent, part, with some of them seeking formal restrictions on the powers of the Shah while others strongly opposed a 'Western-style' constitution.

As befits *mujtahids* with the right of independent interpretation, the ShI'I clergy share a common culture, but they do not speak with one voice. To become a *mujtahid* a student must complete a course in theological studies before receiving written authorization to interpret the law. Having passed this stage he is given the honorary title *hujjat-al-islam* ('proof of Islam'). From the ranks of the *mujtahids*, of whom there are several hundreds, an internal consensus promotes those who have achieved eminence and seniority to the rank of *ayatallah* ('sign of God'). From the ranks of ayatollahs, who will already have their own followings among the theological students, five or six are chosen to become the Grand Ayatollahs who act as 'models to be imitated' (*marja' al-taqlid*). In theory every Shi'a, whether clergy or laity, chooses one *marja'* as his or her religious guide. Given that *marjas* do not always agree with each other on matters of law or politics, the system allows for considerable diversity.

6. Demonstrations following the departure of Shah Mohammed Reza Pahlavi, 20 January 1979. Only a few months previously US President Jimmy Carter described Iran as an 'island of stability' in the Middle East. The mass protests drew heavily on Shi'i themes of martyrdom and sacrifice.

The historical independence of the Shi'i *ulama* was favoured by the fact that two of the most important shrines and centres of Shi'i learning, Karbala (the place of Hussein's martyrdom) and Najaf (mausoleum of 'Ali) lie outside Iran's borders, in the former Ottoman territory of Iraq. The Ottoman rulers were happy to encourage the political independence of the Shi'i clergy *vis-à-vis* their political rivals, the Persian shahs, provided they did not threaten their own interests. The tradition was maintained under the Ottoman Empire's successor-state Iraq which, despite having a population that is at least 55 per cent Shi'i, has a government that remains firmly under Sunni control. In 1963, after mounting a vociferous campaign of opposition to the pro-Western Shah Mohammed Reza Pahlavi's social and agricultural reforms, a senior clergyman from Qum, Ayatollah Ruhallah Khomeini was expelled to Iraq and settled in Najaf. Here, under the benign sufferance of the Iraqi leader Saddam Hussein who had his own quarrels with the Shah, Khomeini was free to preach his doctrine of *Vilayet-e faqih* (the 'governance of the jurist'). This was in effect an argument that in the absence of the Imam the *ulama* had the right, if not the duty, to seize power – following the example of Imam Hussein rather than his elder brother Hasan. Photocopies and audio-cassettes of Khomeini's lectures were smuggled into Iran and widely disseminated among the population. In 1978, on the recommendation of the US Secretary of State Henry Kissinger, who tried to patch up the differences between Iran and Iraq, Khomeini was expelled. He chose to settle near Paris where, by astute manipulation of the international media, he was able to present himself as the Leader in Exile (while secretly engaging in correspondence with the Shah). Unusually for a Shi'i Ayatollah, he allowed himself to be referred to by the title Imam – a title normally reserved for the Twelve holy Imams in succession to the Prophet. While never explicitly claiming to be the Hidden Imam, his informal use of the title and his astute exploitation of the expectations surrounding it undoubtedly furthered his cause. When, in February 1979, following the Shah's departure, Khomeini flew to Tehran, two million people turned up at the airport to greet him. As one of Khomeini's leading opponents, the conservative Ayatollah Shariatmadari, observed: 'No one expected the Hidden Imam to arrive in a Jumbo Jet!'

Khomeini's dominance over the Iranian political scene until his death in 1989 (which saw equally extravagant scenes of mourning, the Imam, as it were, having chosen to go back into hiding) gave the false impression that he spoke for the Iranian clergy as a whole. In fact, two of his most vociferous opponents, the Ayatollahs Shariatmadari (d. 1986) and the popular 'left-wing' Taleqani (d. September 1979), came from the ranks of the senior clergy. In Iraq the Ayatollah Kho'i (1899–1992) remained obstinately non-political (although in 1991 Saddam Hussein forced him to appear on television to denounce the Shi'i uprising in the city of Najaf). Ayatollah Montazeri, whom Khomeini had designated as his successor as supreme guide of the revolution, was later set aside by Khomeini for defending opponents of the revolution and criticizing the death sentence passed on the British author Salman Rushdie. After the collapse of the Shah's regime and the suppression of the Islamic left, it has mainly been the middle-ranking clergy who have benefited from the clerical regime. Many senior clergy remain opposed to Khomeini's idea that the clergy should take an active role in politics. As the clerical government becomes increasingly corrupt and unpopular, it seems probable that the quietist tendency in Shi'ism will reassert itself. The election of the pragmatic *hujjat-ul-islam* Muhammad Khatami to the presidency in May 1997 by a landslide victory against the 'establishment' candidate marked a significant step in this direction. More than two years into his presidency, however, it was apparent that Khatami was far from being in full control of the state. Despite his liberalizing instincts and his desire to end Iran's international isolation – symbolized by his government's formal undertaking to Britain not to implement Khomeini's *fatwa* against Salman Rushdie – Khatami was powerless to prevent the suppression by militias and street gangs controlled by conservative clerics of the pro-democracy student demonstrations that rocked Tehran during the summer of 1999.

Chapter 4

The Shariʿa and its Consequences

Introduction

Just as there is no doctrine of divine incarnation in Islam, so there is no church, no separate institution or body distinct from the rest of society charged with the task of conveying God's will, or the Prophet's teachings, to the ordinary believer. In Islam 'God has not revealed Himself and His nature, but rather His law'. The term Shariʿa applies to much more than law in the strictly legal sense. It includes the details of ritual, as well as a whole range of customs and manners, although local customary laws are also recognized. Shariʿa means literally 'the way to a watering place': the Quranic use of the term suggestively combines the notions of a vital means of sustenance in this world and access to the divine realm of the world to come. The law is there both for the purpose of upholding the good of society and for helping human beings attain salvation. Interpretations of the law may vary in accordance with time and place, but the Shariʿa itself is considered to be a timeless manifestation of the will of God, subject neither to history nor circumstance.

The development of the Shariʿa law was primarily the result of the historic conditions prevailing during Islam's three formative centuries. Coins dating from the reign of ʿAbd al-Malik and some early ʿAbbasid rulers contain the inscription *khalifat Allah* (God's deputy or vice-regent): the early caliphs evidently saw themselves as the divinely appointed fountainheads of law. They based their legal rulings on the Quran, the so-called Sunna of local practice, and decisions based – like those of the Shi'i Imam – on their own divinely inspired insights. Only later did the concept of Sunna come to be applied exclusively to deeds or sayings of the Prophet, as subsequently recorded in the hadith literature. (For example the Caliph 'Umar changed the penalty for adultery from the 100 lashes given in the Quran to stoning – a decision later supported by reference to various hadiths attributed to the Prophet.) In later times the title *khalifat rasul Allah* (deputy of the Messenger of God) came into use, indicating that the Caliph was now seen in a less elevated capacity as the Prophet's Successor. And it is the Prophet whose custom or Sunna looms increasingly large as the primary source of law. The change of nomenclature coincided with the failure of the *mihna* or 'inquisition' which saw the end of the Caliph's attempts to fuse religious and political leadership in his person.

The civil wars and leadership struggles following Muhammad's death eventually limited the Caliph's power and contaminated his authority, leaving no source of authority uncontested save that of the Quran and the Prophet's precepts, embodied in the burgeoning corpus of hadiths. Indeed, the manner in which the Prophet's Sunna eclipses that of the caliphs, as well as that of his Companions and their Successors, closely parallels the development of the Shari'a itself. Local or regional 'living' traditions based on more or less pragmatic judicial decisions of Muslim commanders and the judges they appoint are replaced by more systematic efforts to determine the Will of God, as revealed in the Quran and hadith. The juristic literature through which the Shari'a, God's law or way is elaborated and made explicit is known as *fiqh*, 'knowledge' or 'understanding' (a term often translated by the more technical 'jurisprudence'). Its four roots ('*usul*), in order of precedence, are the Quran, the Prophet's Sunna (as revealed through the hadith literature), *ijma'* or consensus, and *qiyas* (analogical reasoning).

The Roots of Islamic Law

1. Quran

As the direct and unmediated Word of God the Quran is the primary source of law in Islam. In the broadest sense the whole of the Quran is law for Muslims. God proclaims himself in a Book, every single verse of which can be perceived as a divine command. Only a small proportion, however – about 10 per cent of the Quran's 6,000 verses – contains injunctions that can be converted into positive religious or legal requirements. Most of these occur in passages dating from the Madinese period when the Prophet was actively engaged in lawmaking. There are prohibitions on certain foods (pork, carrion, wine, animals slaughtered in pagan ceremonies), a number of legal rules concerning family law (marriage, divorce, and inheritance), criminal law (the *hudud* crimes, including penalties of highway robbery, illicit sexual activity, slander, and wine-drinking), rules about witnesses, and commercial regulations including the ban on *riba* (usury) and forms of contracts. None of these rules is wholly free from ambiguities and lawyers who relied exclusively on the Quran for legislative material would soon find themselves engaged in 'endless debate about whether some verses have been abrogated by others, as most Muslims believe; and if so, which verses were abrogated by which'.

A moral universe

'The Quran is an unparalleled window into the moral universe. It is a source of knowledge in the way that the entire corpus of legal precedent is for the common law tradition: not so much as an index of possible rulings as a quarry in which the astute inquirer can hope to find the building blocks for a morally valid, and therefore, true system of ethics.'

Kevin Reinhart, 'Islamic Law as Islamic Ethics', *Journal of Religious Ethics*, 11/2 (Fall 1983), 189.

2. Sunna

The Prophet's custom as recorded in the hadith literature contains a much larger quantity of legal material than the Quran, based in many cases on the Prophet's own legal judgments. Although Western scholars and some Muslim modernists (like some of the early authorities) have questioned the authenticity of many of these hadiths, the Sunna remains for the vast majority of Muslims the uncontested and uncontestable second root of divine law. The Sunna, however, is very far from being self-explanatory: some hadiths will contradict others, experts will disagree about which are strong and which are weak, and without the two additional 'roots' of law – *ijma'* (consensus) and *qiyas* (analogical reasoning) – coherent legal decision-making would be impossible.

The Muhammadan paradigm

'The *hadith*-reports, considered as a whole, contain the *sunna* of the Prophet, which is not simply a record of the Prophetic doings but of the Prophet's significant, exemplary acts, non-acts, and sayings. The Quran's integrity was guaranteed by its miraculous inimitability and plural transmission; the prophetic *sunna* was vouched for by the immaculate protection ('*isma*) of the Prophet, Quranic attestation, and plural transmission. What is noteworthy is that, except in broad outline, the *sunna* was not a mere catalog of model behaviour to be emulated, but rather a collection of data which required assessment and application in an appropriate context. A life lived totally in accord with the Moral becomes a window into moral knowledge. The Prophet is thus, for the practioner of *fiqh*, not really a model but a normative case, not so much a person as a principle.'

Kevin Reinhart, 'Islamic Law as Islamic Ethics', 190.

3. Ijma'

In the first centuries after the Muslim conquest the scholars who interpreted the law in the different urban centres relied on their own consensus and that of their illustrious predecessors to reach agreement over which hadiths should be accepted and which rejected as sources of law. The idea that *ijma'* should be regarded as a 'root' of jurisprudence was enshrined in a hadith of the Prophet: 'My community will never agree upon an error.' As Muslims would come to see it, *ijma'* was active in the earliest days of Islam when the memory of the Prophet's example was still alive and the community small and culturally homogeneous enough to engage in common practice. Thus the jurist Muhammad b. al-Hasan al-Shaibani (749–805), commenting on a particular legal decision states: 'Whatever the Muslims see as good is good with God, and whatever the Muslims see as bad is bad with God.' For example, circumcision (male and in some areas female) became normative if not universal though it had no sanction other than Arab custom. Hadiths accepted and followed by this early consensus included rulings of the Companions and their Successors as well as those of the Prophet himself. Had Islamic legal development continued along these lines it is probable that a proliferation of regional sects, each claiming for itself universal status, would have resulted. The great Palestinian jurist al-Shafi'i devoted his career to standardizing the law, making sure that the most important hadiths were traced directly to the Prophet. Whereas earlier hadiths might contradict each other, the oral law, like the written law embodied in the Quran, was now believed to come directly from God through the Prophet, and must therefore be free from inconsistencies. The new idea of *ijma'* that crystallized around this doctrine bore the imprint of the consensus of the community as distinct from that of the legal scholars. The Prophet's imprimatur on these legal traditions guaranteed wide if not universal public acceptability. It has been suggested, however, that the creativity and adaptability present during the era of the 'living schools' was accordingly diminished.

Five schools of jurisprudence

In addition to Muhammad ibn Idris al-Shafiʿi (767–820) the four legal schools of Sunni Islam are named after Abu Hanifa (699–767) an Iraqi of Persian extraction, Malik ibn Anas al-Asbahi (713–795) an Arab of Yemeni descent who spent the whole of his life in Medina, leaving it but once to perform the pilgrimage, and Ahmad Ibn Hanbal (780–855) an uncompromising hadith-collector and traditionist who eschewed *ijmaʿ* and used reasoning by analogy only when the Quran, the hadiths and legal rulings of Companions had been exhausted. The Shiʿa have their own school of law, the Jaʿfari school, named after the Sixth Imam, Jaʿfar al Sadiq (see Chapter 4), in which hadiths of ʿAli and the Imams feature prominently alongside those of the Prophet.

Of the four Sunni schools the Hanafi became the most influential, being the official school of the ʿAbbasid caliphs and later of the Ottoman sultans. Today it is the dominant school in religious and family law among the Muslims of the Balkans, Transcaucasia, Afghanistan, Pakistan, India, the central Asian republics, and China. The Maliki school was represented in the Hijaz and spread to the Gulf as well as to Upper Egypt and the Sudan, Andalusia, and north-west Africa, so that it is now the dominant school in Morocco, Algeria, Tunisia, and Libya. The Shafiʿi school is less widely represented than the Hanafi in the Middle East – not least because the Hanafi school displaced it in Egypt after the Ottoman conquest in 1517. Today its followers are to be found mainly in the rural parts of Egypt, Palestine, Jordan, the coastlands of Yemen, and among populations in Pakistan, India, and Indonesia, the world's most populous Muslim country.

4. Qiyas

The fourth of the classical 'roots of jurisprudence' is a form of analogical and syllogistic reasoning similar to the Talmudic *heqqes* from which, some argue, the word has been derived. In principle, it involved the systematic application of logic to situations not explicitly mentioned in the Quran or *hadith*. During the formative period of Islamic law its application was controversial, and some jurists argued against it on the ground that it imputed inadequacy to the Prophet and the Holy Quran. Its defenders, however, cited a *hadith* according to which the Prophet sent one of his companions Mu'adh ibn Jabal to be a judge in Yemen. Before he departed, the Prophet subjected him to a brief interrogation:

> 'How will you reach a judgment when a question arises?'
> 'According to the word of God', replied Muadh.
> 'And if you find no solution in the word of God?'
> 'Then according to the *sunna* of the Messenger of God.'
> 'And if you find no solution in the *sunna* of the Messenger of God nor in the Word?'
> 'Then I shall take a decision according to my own opinion (*rayi*).'

The Prophet was pleased with this answer. He slapped Muadh on the chest, saying 'Praise be to God who has led the Messenger of God to an answer that pleased him'.

The clearest examples of the use of analogical or syllogistic reasoning involves alcoholic drinks. While some jurists would argue that only fermented products of the date-palm and vine are forbidden, others, basing their judgments on *qiyas*, would insist that all alcoholic drinks are forbidden, since the effective cause or common denominator ('*illa*) behind the prohibition was the same in each case: 'All intoxicating drinks count as grape-wine. Vodka is an intoxicating drink. Therefore vodka is forbidden.'

Wine or whisky?

The following is part of a discussion on prohibited liquors from the *Hidaya* of Burhan ul Din al-Marghinani (d. 1197) a Hanafi *faqih* of Farghana in central Asia (modern Uzbekistan). Beer, whisky and vodka, according to this liberal Hanafi view, are permitted, although all forms of grape alcohol are banned absolutely:

'The first of these [forbidden beverages] is *khamr* [wine] meaning, according to Abu Hanifa, the juice of the grape fermented . . . Others maintain that *khamr* is applicable to whatever is of an inebriating quality, because it is mentioned in the traditions that "Whatever inebriates is *khamr*" and in another tradition "*Khamr* is produced from two plants, namely the vine and the date-palm . . ." *Khamr* is in itself unlawful whether it be used . . . even in so small a quantity as not to be sufficient to intoxicate; yet the same law does not apply to other things of an inebriating quality, for a little of them, if not sufficient to intoxicate, is not forbidden . . . Whoever maintains *khamr* to be lawful is an infidel (and exposed to the penalty for apostasy) for he rejects incontestable proof.

'. . . Whoever drinks *khamr* incurs punishment even if he is not intoxicated, for it is said in the Traditions "Let him who drinks *khamr* be whipped, and if he drinks it again, let him be punished again in the same manner."

'Liquor produced by means of honey, wheat, barley or millet is lawful, according to Abu Hanifa and Abu Yusuf (his most distinguished disciple) although it be not boiled, provided it be not drunk in a wanton manner. The argument they adduce is the Hadith "*Khamr* is the product of these two trees" (meaning the vine and the date-palm) . . . It has likewise been disputed whether a person who gets drunk with any of these liquors is to be punished.'

Burhan al Din al-Marghinani, *Al-Hidaya*, tr. Charles Hamilton (2nd edn. London, 1870; Lahore, 1957), 607–8 quoted in Williams, 130.

Religious and social duties

The record of human understanding of the divine will was collated in vast compendia known as the books of *fiqh*. These books are not legal codes, but they do offer guidance for judges. The typical *fiqh* manual is divided into religious and social duties (*'ibadat* and *mu'amalat*). The section on *'ibadat* will focus primarily on the five *rukns* or 'pillars' (see Appendix). It will have detailed prescriptions about ablutions, the times and exact performance of prayer both privately and on Friday, the Day of Congregation; *zakat* (compulsory charity); the Ramadan fast, and the pilgrimage to Makka.

Mu'amalat are the laws governing human relationships; in their modern application they are largely confined to questions of personal status, marriage, and inheritance as well as prohibitions on forbidden substances such as pork or wine. They also include political matters such as the theory of the caliphate which in classical times fell within the active purview of the Shari'a.

Ijtihad: The Struggle for Truth

Legal reasoning by analogy and syllogism was one aspect of the effort (*ijtihad*) needed to fathom the law as revealed by God and his Prophet. The word *ijtihad* shares the same root as *jihad* ('struggle') – a term usually translated as 'holy war'. The jurist must exhaust himself intellectually in order to determine the details of God's command. *Ijtihad*, in the words of one authority, involves 'the total expenditure of effort in the search for an opinion as to any legal rule in such a manner that the individual senses (within himself) an inability to expend further effort'. The goal is not law making, but *fiqh* – understanding or knowledge of a law deemed to exist already.

The Shari'a is divine, co-eternal with God. *Fiqh*, by contrast, is the product of human endeavour. The *faqih* – one who practises *fiqh* – is a legal specialist who seeks through exercising *ijtihad* to reach conclusions about the Shari'a, to determine the implications of God's commands in particular instances. If he is unable to exercise *ijtihad*, he should use another method known as *taqlid* – the imitation of a recognised *mujtahid*. For if everyone exercised personal *ijtihad*, the result would be chaos. In the course of time the jurists became increasingly reluctant to practise *ijtihad*, preferring to rely on *taqlid*. Juridical loyalties crystallized around the four leading figures credited with founding the four main legal schools (*madhabs*) of Sunni Islam.

The differences between the four legal schools of Sunni Islam are mainly confined to questions such as marriage and guardianship, with the Hanafis taking a more liberal view of female rights than the Malikis. Legal differences between the Sunni schools and Shi'i Ja'fari school are not very great. There are small differences in the ritual of prayer. The most significant are in the laws of inheritance and in an institution known as *muta'* (Persian *sigheh*) or temporary marriage (see Chapter 5). Although jurists from all schools with the exception of the Hanbalis continued to exercise *ijtihad* for many centuries, the doctrine emerged that the 'gates of *ijtihad*' had been closed after the third Muslim century. Recent scholarship, however, suggests that the gates were never closed completely, and that famous *mujtahids* in the Sunni tradition continued to practise at least until the sixteenth century CE.

In Shi'i jurisprudence the 'gates of *ijtihad*' are generally assumed to have remained open. Senior Shi'i *ulama* known by the title of hujjat al-Islam ('proof of Islam') or Ayatullah ('sign of God') are all *mujtahids* – individual interpreters of the law. Every believing Shi'i is supposed to place him or herself under the guidance of a *mujtahid* who acts as a 'source of imitation' (*marja-it-aqlid* in Persian). The Shi'i *ulama* are the recipients of religious taxes (*zakat* and *khums*) and historically this has given them more independence of government than their Sunni counterparts. The autonomy of the religious establishment *vis-à-vis* the state makes it an 'estate' comparable to the Christian clergy or Buddhist Sangha. The independent network of mosques allied to the traditional business sector (the 'bazaar') enabled the Iranian religious establishment to take power through its political wing, the Islamic Republican Party, during the events that accompanied the collapse of the Pahlavi dynasty in the winter of 1978–9 (see Chapter 6).

The intellectual and hermeneutical flexibility of the Shi'i *'ulama* have given them the edge over their Sunni counterparts in adapting the law to contemporary circumstances. Where Sunni Islamists have actively sought political power, it has often been freelancers or religious auto-didacts who have made the running. Where scholarly-trained individuals, such as Shaikh 'Ali Ben Hadj of Algeria or Shaikh 'Umar 'Abd al-Rahman of Egypt, have become involved in political or terrorist activity, it has not been in their capacities as members of the religious establishment, but rather as charismatic individuals. In the Sunni tradition the *fiqh* began to calcify within its own intellectual sphere, becoming increasingly divorced from the realities of the vast and diverse domains acquired by Muhammad's successors. Al-Shafi'i's insistence – adopted by the other *madhabs* – on pinning as many legal rulings as possible to the Prophet's example ensured a remarkable degree of uniformity, though local and regional customs inevitably persisted – often under the guise of hadiths of doubtful authenticity. This is not to say, however, that the system was monolithic. There remained considerable diversity within the corpus of Islamic jurisprudence as it developed, the variations justified by reference to another important hadith: 'The differences between the learned of my community are a blessing from God.'

The Shari'a: An all-encompassing Ideal

The books of *fiqh* divide human conduct into five categories which cover everything 'from murder to social etiquette, and from incest to the rules of religious retreat'. The categories in the varied terminology of the jurists comprise the things that are commanded, recommended, left legally indifferent, disapproved of, and forbidden. The formulation involved the explicit rejection of the view advocated by the Mu'tazila that the moral world could be divided into the bipolar categories of good and evil. The fivefold system represents the compromise made in the first two centuries between the moral perfectionism of early Muslim communities such as the Kharijis, and the demands of an expanding Islamic community that aimed to be inclusive and universal.

In principle this remarkably comprehensive scheme allows no ultimate distinction between religion and morality, law and ethics. All are seen as proceeding directly from the command of God, though there is room for humans to argue about the details. Only God can judge the extent to which an individual's activities conform to the jurists' schema. Law in the narrower sense is restricted to dealing with those activities that are explicitly forbidden (*haram*) or to adjudicating between competing claims of individuals.

Western legal historians tend to argue that the Shari'a developed as an ideal system of law divorced from practice. The mainly oral procedure and high standards of proof – though admirable for protecting the rights of accused persons in relatively small communities such as the Prophet's Medina – were less appropriate in the expanding cosmopolitan societies of the Arab empire. Strictures against *riba* (lending and borrowing at fixed rates of interest) were widely evaded by legal devices, making whole areas of commercial law impossible to enforce. As a consequence the administration of criminal justice was never fully entrusted to the *qadis*. The *qadi* courts were supplemented by those of the police, while the *muhtasib*, the Inspector of Markets – a lineal descendant of the Byzantine *agronomos* – took a vast range of commercial practice under his wing. Where they found the Shari'a rules inadequate, inappropriate, or limiting the rulers added their own supplementary decrees and enforced laws other than the Shari'a in the *mazalim* courts, the rulers' Courts of Complaints.

Five categories of behaviour

The classical lawbooks divide all human behaviour into five categories:

1. Required, obligatory (*wajib* or *fard*) 'for the neglect of which one ought to be punished (both in this world and in the hereafter) and for the doing of which one is rewarded'. Obligations are divided into *fard 'ain*, individual duties, such as prayer, almsgiving and fasting; and *fard kifaya*, collective duties, such as attendance at funeral prayers or participation in the jihad or holy war.

2. Proscribed or prohibited (*mahzur, haram*), acts 'for the performance of which there is punishment and (according to most authorities) for the avoidance of which there is reward'. The punishment is usually inflicted in this world according to Islamic law. Categories include certain types of theft, illicit sexual activity, wine drinking – the so-called *hudud* offences – for which specific penalties are prescribed in the Quran. The rewards for abstention are presumed to be in paradise.

3. Recommended (*mandub, masnun, mustahhab, sunna*): acts that are commendable but not required, 'for the doing of which there is reward, but for the neglect of which there is no punishment'. They include charitable acts such as the manumission of slaves, supererogatory prayers and fasts, pious deeds of all varieties.

4. Discouraged or odious (*makruh*), 'acts for the doing of which there is no punishment, but for the avoidance of which there is reward'. There is wide disagreement about this category but some authorities would include divorce, permitted by unilateral male declaration, but disapproved of by the Prophet.

5. Permitted but morally indifferent (*jaiz, mubah*), 'acts for the performance or avoidance of which there is neither reward nor punishment'.

The judge's role

An American legal anthropologist who attended sessions of a Moroccan Shari'a court over several years observed:

'Rather than being aimed simply at the invocation of state or religious power . . . the aim of the *qadi* is to put people back in the position of being able to negotiate their own permissible relationships without predetermining just what the outcome of those negotiations ought to be . . . Even the social interest is conceptualized in terms of maintaining private interaction: what is good for the individual is good for society. What is missing, until at least the beginning of western influence, is the institutionalization of the public as an entity whose interests might be assessed like those of a person. In the absence of the idea that corporate entities might constitute jural personalities the social interest enters the law as a localized interpretation of the legal status of particular named persons and their highly personalized acts.'

Lawrence Rosen, *The Anthropology of Justice: Law as Culture in Islamic Society* (Cambridge: Cambridge University Press, 1989), 17, 49.

The Shari'a and Muslim Societies

By defining correct behaviour or orthopraxy at the social level, the Shari'a has left its distinctive imprint on a way of living that has evolved over time and varies from one country to another in accordance with local custom.

As well as sanctioning sexual inequality (see Chapter 5), the laws of inheritance prevented concentrations of wealth among individuals, as

7. Aerial view of Damascus showing the labyrinthine density of the streets in the old city. In the absence of a formally constituted public domain, the streets were constantly subject to private encroachments.

estates had to be divided according to the provisions of the Shari'a which limits the amount a single heir may inherit while favouring a multiplicity of claims by agnatic kin (relatives in the male line). Although these provisions could be evaded by the creation of family trusts (*awqaf*), endowments from which the founders' families could draw incomes in perpetuity, such provisions militated against the productive use of capital for commercial and industrial purposes.

The Shari'a, both in theory and practice, was uncompromisingly individualistic. The absence of the concept of church – the mystical 'body of Christ' that stood between the individual Christian and God through which alone salvation was possible – militated against the creation of institutions such as the medieval Western city or trading company where the group interest transcended that of the individual. The Shari'a recognized no corporate entities which could be treated as persons in law. The purpose of the law, apart from enforcing God's commands, was to regulate the affairs of men. One consequence of the absence of the concept of jural personality of groups may be seen in the proliferating alleyways of many pre-modern Middle East cities, where private territory – cafés, workshops, stalls, and so forth – constantly encroaches on public space. The public domain, it is presumed, is simply the sum of its private components, not a separate entity requiring legal protection. The positive result is a law that is primarily directed at social self-regulation. The Muslim judge, like the ancient hadith collector, must be above all a judge of persons. In the words of a Saudi Arabian scholar, he must have 'an acute sense of observation: for example just by looking at a suspect he should be able to tell what the man has concealed in his testimony'. In traditional Muslim societies the 'science of men' administered by the judge provided the connecting link between divine justice and the human environment in which it was supposed to operate. The idealism of the Shari'a was mitigated by a humane and humanistic pragmatism.

A negative consequence of the Shari'a approach to law has been the

Law as common sense

'Islamic law . . . seeks consistency with common-sense assumptions about humanity, not through the refinement of categories of its own creation. [It] is a system of adjudication, of ethics and of logic that finds its touchstone not in the perfecting of doctrine, but in the standards of everyday life, and measured in this way it is enormously developed, integrated, logical and successful. Man's duty is to conform to God's moral limits, not to try to invent them. But within the limits established by God one can create relationships and traffic in the knowledge of their existence, intricacies and repercussions.'

Rosen, *The Anthropology of Justice*, 56.

lack of legitimacy accorded the public interest in the form of city, state, or any other institution standing between the individual and God. Corruption is endemic in many societies, and it would be unfair to target Muslim societies as being uniquely prone to bribery, graft, and the private misappropriation of public funds. Patrimonialism – the confusion of private and public realms – is rife in developing countries. However, a culture informed by the absence of institutional boundaries between the public and private spheres may be more vulnerable to such abuses than one where the boundaries are rigorously upheld by law. In Western societies these boundaries are part of the historical residue of medieval Christendom, with its separate distribution of powers between church and state. 'Family values' including those of the extended kinship group are fundamental to Shari'a and, where family values predominate, the state is vulnerable to manipulation by powerful family networks. Yet the idealism implicit in the Shari'a, the utopian expectations it engenders, militates against the constitutional limitation of power. It is pessimism about human nature (a by-product, arguably, of the Christian doctrine of original sin) that leads to the liberal perception that all power corrupts, and that constitutional limitations must be placed on its exercise.

This personalized or individualized nature of the Shari'a has not merely given its application an intimate and personal character – a character that is, arguably, reinforced, by the application of public corporal punishments including flogging and execution, for certain categories of crime. It traps the modern Islamist political discourse in what might be called a 'virtuous circle'. Rather than addressing systemic or institutional reform, modern Islamist reformers like Maududi have simply stressed a 'return' to the Shari'a, placing an excessive degree of emphasis on personal virtue. As the French scholar Olivier Roy points out, because the Islamist model is predicated on the belief in government by morally impeccable individuals who can be counted on to resist temptation, it does not generate institutions capable of functioning autonomously by means of structural checks and balances. Political institutions function only as a result of the virtue of those who run them, but virtue can become widespread only if society is already Islamic.

Chapter 5
Women and Family

Introduction

No subject is more fraught with controversy than the relation of women
and Islam. On one side of the debate there exists the widespread
perception that the faith oppresses and even persecutes women; at the
other there are arguments about cultural authenticity, about the rights
of women to assert themselves in ways that differ from the modes of
female self-assertion current in non-Muslim societies. The issue is
complicated by the interaction of history, religion, culture, and politics.
Historically the patriarchal family and the extended networks of kinship
connected with it have proved to be among the most durable social
structures in Muslim societies, far more durable than structures built
around professional association or class interest. The role of religion in
sustaining these structures is not entirely clear. Islamic law privileges
the family over other institutions: the laws of inheritance, favouring
males over females, are written in the Quran along with other
discriminatory provisions, such as the testamentary inferiority of
females in certain court proceedings. The law, however, is not always a
reliable guide to actual social practice: slavery and concubinage, widely
practised in pre-colonial times, are also the subject of detailed legal
provisions and though permitted under the Shariʿa, both have
disappeared (in theory if not always in practice) from Muslim societies.
Unlike the *hijab* or 'veil' they are not among the shibboleths insisted
upon by today's Islamists.

Protection of the patriarchal family and the symbolic capital it holds in the shape of female chastity is deeply embedded in the semantics of Islam: the word *haram* (sacred, forbidden, taboo) shares the same root with *harim* – the part of the household reserved for women – and *mahram* – the kinship group to which a woman is forbidden sexually by law, and within which she is free to associate. The duality of the manifest and the hidden (*al-shahada/al-ghaib, al-zahir/al-batin*), fundamental to the Quranic approach to the divine, is suggestively linked in at least one passage to sexuality, with the female pudenda associated with the hidden aspect of deity. Restrictions on women are intimately bound up with notions of the sacred. As Michael Gilsenan has observed of village life in northern Lebanon, *sharaf*, 'the honour of person and family which is particularly identified with control of women's sexuality, is crucial to the public, social identity of men'. The same observation applies, *a fortiori,* in many other parts of the Muslim world. But an obsession with gender and status and its corollary, the assertion of masculine power through violence, is by no means exclusively Islamic. The same patriarchal assumptions are found in non-Muslim Mediterranean societies as well as others further afield. Conversely there are Muslim communities in West Africa and south-east Asia where matrilineal systems of ownership and inheritance predominate. All of this calls into question the view that Islamic texts and the values they enshrine are of themselves responsible for types of behaviour underpinning male supremacism. At the same time there can be no doubt that the public and symbolic role of women lies at the heart of the Islamist discourse. In one polemic after another Islamist writers contrast the virtuous Muslim woman with her Western or Westernized counterpart – naked, unchaste, and corrupt, a potent source of *fitna* or strife.

Women and the Shariʿa

As with other politically charged issues in contemporary Islam the debate surrounding the veil is fuelled by diverging perspectives upon an

Spiritual equality

Men and women who have surrendered,
believing men and believing women,
obedient men and obedient women,
truthful men and truthful women,
humble men and humble women,
men and women who give in charity,
men who fast and women who fast,
men and women who guard their private parts,
men and women who remember God oft –
for them God has prepared forgiveness and a mighty wage.
(Quran 33: 35)

exemplary past. Traditionalists, most of them men, argue that the Prophet of Islam greatly improved the position of the Arabian women of his time, guaranteeing them basic rights in marriage that were denied to the women of the time of ignorance – the *jahiliya*. Makkan suras of the Quran refer with abhorrence to the custom of female infanticide and the neglect of widows and orphans. After Islam women were given guaranteed rights of inheritance under the protective umbrella of the family. A woman's husband was obligated to provide for her and her children. Although polygyny (one man and a plurality of wives) was permitted the man was limited to four wives, each of whom had to be treated equally. No spiritual inequality is implied. The Quran explicitly addresses itself to females as well as males and morally women will be as answerable for their actions on the Day of Judgement as men.

That said, however, there are particular verses which testify to the legal inferiority of women. A sister shares only half the portion of her brothers under the Quranic laws of inheritance – the assumption being that her husband will maintain her. A husband may physically chastise a

Male authority

*'Your women are a tillage for you; so come
unto your tillage as you wish, and forward
for your souls; and fear God, and know that
you shall meet Him . . .'*
(Quran 2: 224)

*'Men are the managers of the affairs of women
for that God has preferred in bounty
one of them over another, and for that
they have expended of their property.
Righteous women are therefore obedient
guarding the secret for God's guarding.
And those you fear may be rebellious
admonish; banish them to their couches,
and beat them. If they then obey you,
look not for any way against them; God is
All-high, All-great.'*
(Quran 4: 35)

'Whenever the Prophet (peace be on him) permitted a man to administer corporal punishment to his wife, he did so with reluctance, and continued to express his distaste for it. And even in cases where it is necessary, the Prophet (peace be on him) directed men not to hit across the face, nor to beat severely nor to use anything that might leave marks on the body.'

From Maududi's commentary on Quran 4: 35 in Sayyid Abu'l `Ala Maududi, *Tafhim al-Quran*, tr. and ed. Zafar Ishaq Ansari (Leicester: Islamic Foundation, 1989), ii, 36.

recalcitrant or disobedient wife as a final resort when other measures have failed. In certain legal proceedings a woman's testimony is only worth half that of a man: it is assumed that she will be unfamiliar with business matters and that she will need a friend to jog her memory. In the context of seventh-century Arabia these Quranic rubrics are not necessarily incompatible with the argument that Islam substantially improved the status of women, not least by improving their security in marriage and property. Modern feminists wishing to move beyond these positions, however, face a theological obstacle. As the unalterable speech of God the Quran is deemed to be non-negotiable: for the majority of Muslims, the spirit is firmly anchored in the letter. To argue that modern conditions demand an end to the Quran's discriminatory provisions is to challenge the dogma that the text is fixed for eternity. Feminist writers are forced by the logic of their position to de-couple the text from the spirit in favour of a flexible doctrine that leads inevitably to the recontextualization of Islam's holy book. The issue of women's rights is inexorably caught up in the issue of modernism.

As modernists see it, the Quran was revealed at a specific time and in a specific social context. Their task is to reinterpret the spirit of its provisions in the light of modern realities. The difficulty facing modernists is that those who take the text at face value, refusing to deconstruct it to suit current social trends or fashions, are often closer to its original meaning and purpose. To take a well-known example, the verses allowing polygyny require that each wife be treated equally. Traditionalists interpreted equality in legalistic terms: the right of each wife to her own household, to equality of material provision. Modernists undermine the whole institution by adding an emotional and psychological dimension to the notion of equality, arguing that since no man can be expected to be equally emotionally involved with all his wives, polygyny is effectively ruled out.

Similar arguments are deployed by modernists to rationalize the

Two verses on polygamy

'marry such women
as seem good to you, two, three, four;
but if you fear you will not be equitable,
then only one, or what your right hands own (i.e. slave-girls).'
(Quran 4: 3)

'Some people who have been overwhelmed and overawed by the Christianized outlook of Westerners have tried to prove that the real aim of the Quran was to put an end to polygamy (which, in their opinion, is intrinsically evil). Since it was widely practised at that time, however, Islam confined itself to placing restrictions on it. Such arguments only show the mental slavery to which these people have succumbed. That polygamy is an evil per se is an unacceptable proposition, for under certain conditions it becomes a moral and social necessity. If polygamy is totally prohibited men who cannot remain satisfied with only one wife will look outside the bounds of matrimonial life and create sexual anarchy and corruption. This is likely to cause much greater harm than polygamy to the moral and social order. For this reason the Quran has allowed those who feel the need for it to resort to polygamy.'

Maududi, *Tafhim al-Quran*, ii, 7–8: commentary on Quran 4: 3.

'It [co-wife] is a terrible word – my pen almost halts in writing it – women's mortal enemy . . . How many hearts has it broken, how many minds has it confused and homes destroyed, how much evil brought and how many innocents sacrificed and prisoners taken for whom it was the origin of personal calamity? . . . [It is] a terrible word laden with savagery and selfishness . . . Bear in mind that as you amuse yourself with your new bride you cause another's despair to flow in tears . . . and

96

draconian punishments against unfaithful wives or individuals accused
of illicit sexual activity (*zina*). Under the strict Quranic rules of evidence,
the crime of *zina* must be attested by four independent adult male
witnesses to the act itself. Since in the nature of things such a provision
is almost impossible to satisfy, according to this argument sexual
propriety is satisfied in principle while intrusive social censoriousness is
avoided. Thus Leila Badawi draws attention to legal interpretations that
appear liberal by pre-modern standards: in the case of a deserted or
widowed woman who becomes pregnant she may be protected by the
legal fiction (*hila*) of the 'sleeping foetus', according to which a
pregnancy can be accepted as lasting five or even seven years, while the
child remains the legal heir of the dead or absent husband. An
unmarried woman who becomes pregnant can resort to the fiction of
the 'public bath'. Baths were traditionally opened on alternating days or
hours for men and women, and a virgin, it was claimed, who visited the
public baths after the men had just vacated them might inadvertently
sit on a pool of semen thereby making herself pregnant.

If theory is sometimes harsher than practice in upholding marital
fidelity, the converse can apply with regard to inheritance. In many
Muslim lands women have been systematically denied their inheritance
rights under Islamic law, either by family pressures or by legal devices
such as the family *waqf* or trust. Marriage between first cousins,
permitted under Islamic law, is often converted into a positive

Women and Family

Sukayna's example

'[Sukayna] made one of her husbands sign a marriage contract that officially specified her right to *nushuz*, that rebellion against marital control that so tormented the *fuqaha* [pl. of *faqih*]. She claimed the right to be *nashiz*, and paraded it, like her beauty and her talent, to assert the importance and vitality of women in the Arab tradition. Admiring and respectful, the historians delight in evoking her family dramas – for instance, the case she brought against one of her husbands who had violated the rule of monogamy that she had imposed on him in the marriage contract. Dumbfounded by the conditions in the contract, the judge nevertheless was obliged to hear the case, with his own wife attending this trial of the century and the caliph sending him an emissary to keep him au courant with the course of the trial.'

Fatima Mernissi, *Women and Islam: An Historical and Theological Enquiry*, tr. Mary Jo Lakeland (Oxford: Blackwell, 1991), 192.

injunction, with girls obliged to marry their first cousins. The aim of such customs has been to keep property in the patriarchal family, countering the distributive effects of the laws of inheritance which allow women to inherit a portion of their parents' wealth.

Marriage in Islam is contractual, and given that contracts are negotiable, reformers and modernizers have argued that legal imbalances can be countered by specific contractual provisions, for instance, by following the example of the Prophet Muhammad's great-granddaughter Sukayna bint Hussein who stipulated that her husband remain monogamous. However not all the legal schools accept the woman's right to set the terms of the contract in this way and in any case her ability to do so is likely to be contingent on the power and status of her family. Just as in modern Pakistan it is not the women from upper-class families who suffer from harassment in the market, not least because they are driven around by male chauffeurs, so aristocratic women like Sukayna were spared the insecurities and indignities experienced by lower-class women.

Marriage and Divorce

Marriage is positively enjoined in Islam, and young people are urged to marry with the explicit objective of avoiding exposure to sexual temptation. 'Young men, those of you who can support a wife should marry, for it keeps you from looking at women and preserves your chastity' says one of al-Bukhari's hadiths. Under the Shari'a the marriage contract – *nikah* – is a legal contract sanctioned by the divine law. It is not, as in Christianity, a sacrament. According to most legal authorities the woman's *wali* or guardian (usually her father) enters into the marriage on her behalf and most agree that a virgin may be forced to marry a man of her father's choice. Only the Shi'ia view the woman 'as a full legal entity coequal with her male counterpart'. A Muslim woman's interest is supposed to be secured by the *mahr* or dowry provided by her husband, a sum of money or its equivalent in household goods and chattels, which remains in her possession should her husband initiate divorce.

The husband has the right of divorce by *talaq* – repudiation or unilateral declaration. He must pronounce the formula 'I divorce you' three times; the first two declarations are followed by the so-called *idda*, or waiting period of three menstrual cycles to ensure that the woman is free from pregnancy, or, if pregnant, to ensure the husband's paternity. During this period family and friends are encouraged to effect a reconciliation. If this fails the third declaration finalizes the divorce, without recourse to a court. A man will usually have custody of his children beyond the age of 7 for boys or 9 for girls. If the wife initiates divorce, a procedure

The submissive wife

'It is not lawful for a woman who believes in Allah to allow anyone in her husband's house while he dislikes it. She should not go out of the house if he dislikes it and should not obey anyone who contradicts his orders. She should not refuse to share his bed [meaning that she should not deny him sexual access when he desires it – Trans.]. She should not beat him (in case she is stronger than he). If he is more in the wrong than she, she should plead with him until he is reconciled. If he accepts her pleading well and good, and her plea will be accepted by Allah; while if he is not reconciled with her, her plea will have reached Allah in any case.'

Hadith reported by al-Hakim, quoted in Qaradawi, 204.

known as *khul'*, she sacrifices her *mahr* or dowry. Muslim men are permitted to marry non-Muslim women from the People of the Book – i.e. Jews and Christians. The reverse does not apply. Contemporary Muslim writers such as Dr Yusuf al-Qaradawi argue that the lack of symmetry in this respect is based on the presumption that the man is head of the household. Whereas Muslims are bound to respect the religious rights of Christian and Jewish wives there is no guarantee that Jewish or Christian husbands will safeguard a Muslim wife's freedom of worship. Other observers, however, see the rule as an unambiguous assertion of Muslim supremacism. A Lebanese anthropologist, Fuad Khuri, notes that the same pattern, whereby the dominant caste allows its sons but not its daughters to marry outside the group, prevails among Lebanon's divided communities. Where Shi'ia predominate Shi'i men may marry Sunni women, but not vice versa; where Sunnis are dominant, the converse applies. Similar rules used to apply to riding animals, with the dominant group allowing itself the use of horses while the subordinate group is restricted to riding mules and donkeys, the heights of houses where dominion is expressed architecturally, and clothes, with the dominant groups wearing sober colours – bright colours being associated with children and lower status groups.

Temporary Marriage

Patriarchal assumptions pervade the Shariʿa as interpreted by most traditionalists. A man's right to sexual satisfaction is divinely instituted: the wife does not have the right to refuse her husband's sexual demands. Among the Twelver Shiʿa men's sexual privileges are taken a stage further, with the temporary marriage contract (*mutʿa* or *sigheh*), which may be signed for a fixed period of time ranging from one hour to ninety-nine years. While critics see the institution as a form of legalized prostitution, leading figures in the Islamic Republic of Iran have actively promoted it, arguing that it constitutes 'an ethically and morally superior alternative to the "free" relations between the sexes prevalent in the West'.

Islam and Sexuality

'There is no monkery in Islam,' runs a well-known hadith. 'Copulate and procreate', runs another 'for I shall gain glory from your numbers at the Day of Judgement.' Unlike the virginal Jesus the Prophet of Islam is celebrated as enjoying not just the company of women but the pleasures of sex. After Khadija's death he is said to have married at least nine women, possibly as many as thirteen. Hadiths proclaim his virility: one in al-Bukhari's collection claims he had intercourse with nine of his wives in a single night. Christian polemicists used such images to depict the Prophet as a monster of sensuality. Modern Muslim apologists have reacted defensively, insisting that Muhammad's marriages were either political – aimed at cementing tribal alliances – or designed to provide social security for the women, several of whom were widows. While both these explanations are convincing in the context of a pastoral nomadic society where polygyny was the norm they need not exclude

A foretaste of paradise

'Sexual desire as a manifestation of God's wisdom has, independently of its manifest function, another function: when the individual yields to it and satisfies it, he experiences a delight which would be without match if it were lasting. It is a foretaste of the delights secured for men in Paradise, because to make a promise to men of delights they have not tasted would be ineffective . . . This earthly delight, imperfect because limited in time, is a powerful motivation to incite men to try and attain the perfect delight, the eternal delight, and therefore urges men to adore God so as to reach heaven. Therefore the desire to reach the heavenly delight is so powerful that it helps men to persevere in pious activities in order to be admitted to heaven.'

Abu Hamid al-Ghazali, *ihya ulum al din* ('Revivification of the Religious Sciences') (Cairo n.d.), 27, cited in Fatima Mernissi, *Beyond the Veil: Male-Female Dynamics in Modern Muslim Society* (rev. edn. London: Al Saqi Books, 1985) 29.

the image of Muhammad as the ideal typical charismatic leader, a figure classically associated with sexual prowess. (Another example is the polygamous Mormon Prophet Joseph Smith.) However, the presence of such stories in the literature probably tells us as much about the expectations surrounding leadership as anything that can be factually determined about Muhammad's personal predilections. His sexuality, like that of Christ, opens up a range of interpretative possibilities. Setting aside the historical question, his multiple marriages testify to a positive attitude towards human sexuality which contrasts strikingly with the asceticism of the early Christian Church. At the core of its vision, according to the Tunisian scholar Abdelwahab Bouhdiba, Islam reflects a 'lyrical view of life'. The pleasures of sex are a foretaste of paradise as described in the Quran and elaborated by the exegetes into the 'infinite orgasm' – the state of ecstasy that ultimately leads to the beatific vision and union with God. In the post-Freudian age language and images that appalled and disgusted Christians of a more prudish era deserve to be appreciated for the life-affirming message they impart.

Women in Social and Religious Life

In the classical traditions the positive value of sexuality is affirmed, but it is also perceived as dangerous and potentially destructive of the social order determined by God. The bias against celibacy prevents the emergence of a distinctive caste of female religious comparable to the nuns and abbesses of the Christian West. The sense that good social order is contingent on regulating sexuality – particularly female sexuality – becomes institutionalized. The seclusion of women is justified by fear of female sexual power: an atavistic cultural memory, perhaps, of the female deities destroyed by the prophet of triumphant singular God.

Gender differences are strongly emphasized, God having created humans male and female, and any aspect of behaviour in dress or comportment that clouds the distinction is discouraged or forbidden. Homosexuality, in this view, is a major sin, 'a reversal of the natural order, a corruption of man's sexuality and a crime against the rights of females'. Men should grow beards in order to distinguish themselves from infidels. 'Be different from the polytheists,' says a hadith in al-Bukhari's collection: 'let the beard grow and trim the mustache.' It is makruh (disapproved of) to shave the beard or drastically to cut or shorten it, but it is mustahab (commendable) 'to remove something from its length and breadth if it grows big'.

Apart from her husband, if she is married, a woman's social circle must be confined, according to traditional interpretations of the law, to female friends and her *mahrams* – which includes those male members of her extended family whom she cannot marry by law. These are fathers, sons, brothers, foster-brothers, nephews, and male in-laws. Although local customs vary the taboo on female association with men outside the *mahram* relationship is widespread in Muslim societies from Morocco to South Asia. These patterns, however, are not universal. In parts of Africa south of the Sahara Islamic law has become mixed with local traditions giving women substantially greater rights in marriage and divorce. Among Muslims in South East Asia there are no traditions of seclusion and elements of matrilineal customs survive even in pious communities. Here the Shari'a is seen in terms of religious and ethical duties (*'ibadat*) rather than social practices (*mu'amalat*), where local customary law has priority.

In the Middle East and South Asia and other parts of the Muslim world the extended kinship group sustained by the *mahram* taboo was basic to the social structure. The contrast with the development of Western societies is striking. In the medieval West the Church sustained deliberate policies against kin-based groups, encouraging distance-marriages, insisting that the Church as the corporate body of Christ transcend and supercede the biological ties of kinship. As the Church was gradually replaced by civil bodies, from cities to trading corporations, class interests and divisions emerged which in due course became the occasion of social conflicts and hence the subject of historical change. Women's emancipation was predicated on the emancipation of *men* from the bonds of kinship, with profession, trade, or class eventually acting as co-determinants of an individual's identity along with 'family background'. There being no church in Islam to compete with the family as focus of allegiance, the individual remained much more closely tied to the bonds of kinship. Women may sometimes have enjoyed an honoured and protected position in this system, but their freedom was limited in proportion to their reproductive capacity as genetic carriers and bearers of kinship identity. Today the legacy of the privileged status the family had under the

8. Detail of *mashrabiya*, Cairo. These wooden lattice overhangs, a familiar feature of pre-modern domestic architecture in the Middle East, enhanced ventilation while ensuring female privacy.

Shari'a continues to militate against the assertion of alternative institutions or solidarities based on free association or common purpose. In many Muslim countries, public institutions have been subverted or undermined by the persistence of kinship solidarities: examples are the ruling Ba'ath (Renaissance) parties in Syria and Iraq, both of which are dominated by kinship groups from sectarian minorities.

The exclusion of women from the public domain in the main Islamic centres inevitably led to their exclusion from the religious domain as well. In Cairo, for example – as described by Edward Lane in the 1820s – women were forbidden to pray alongside men in the mosques because 'the Muslims are of the opinion that the presence of females inspires a very different kind of devotion from that which is requisite in a place dedicated to the worship of God'. Female exclusion was reinforced by pollution taboos over menstruation, childbirth, and contact with young children. The hadith collections contain detailed sections on ritual impurities, and it is generally women who are disadvantaged by the rules. Women participate in some Sufi practices and are often associated with visits to the tombs of saints or 'friends' of God – activities often disapproved of by the 'ulama. In the more tradition-bound sections of society female religiosity is more likely to find expression in activities disapproved of by the pious, such as the zar or spirit possession cults still widespread in Egypt and North Africa. Significantly, these spirits are now said to be forcing their 'hosts' to resist the veil: baladi (country) women ordered to cover themselves in accordance with Islamist demands are 'possessed' by spirits which cause them to fall sick if they do so.

Women, Colonialism, and the Family

The collapse of the majority of the world's Muslim states before European military power during the colonial era made the family the primary refuge of Muslim identity. 'Men often ridiculed and rejected in the new colonial governmental and economic structures, found their families a sanctuary, a representation of Islamic religious values wherein they were honoured.' If the family was a sacred area, relatively free from the humiliations imposed by colonial overlords, the woman was its centre, 'the hub around which all its economic, personal and political activities revolved'. Family law was the core of the Shari'a: because of its sacred resonances, reforming governments were reluctant to tamper with it, despite changes introduced in the areas of civil, commercial, and penal law. When reforms were introduced they were perceived by traditionalists as coming from a hostile West. Wealthy women such as Hoda Sharawi in Egypt were the first to throw off the veil, a symbol of oppression for emancipated upper-class women, but for others a symbol of cultural authenticity. As the upper classes, encouraged by colonial administrations who saw veiling as oppressive, adopted European dress and manners, so they were perceived as having abandoned Islamic tradition, identity, and family values.

Family values

'The Muslim family is the miniature of the whole of Muslim society and its firm basis. In it the man or father functions as the imam in accordance with the patriarchal nature of Islam. The religious responsibility of the family rests upon his shoulders ... In the family the father upholds the tenets of the religion and his authority symbolizes that of God in the world. The man is in fact respected in the family precisely because of the sacerdotal function that he fulfils. The rebellion of Muslim women in certain quarters of Islamic society came when men themselves ceased to fulfil their religious function and lost their virile and patriarchal character. By becoming themselves effeminate they caused the ensuing reaction of revolt among certain women who no longer felt the authority of religion upon themselves.'

Seyyed Hossein Nasr, *Ideals and Realities of Islam* (London: George Allen & Unwin, 1966; repr. 1975), 110.

Sartorial Politics

Costume and physical appearance in pre-modern societies was never a matter of purely personal choice. In the West until quite recently dress was the primary external indicator of status, class, and trade. Dress codes still play an important part in many educational institutions and uniforms are an essential component of the corporate identities many firms still impose on their employees. In Muslim societies, where specialist crafts and skills were often the preserve of particular ethnic groups, dress and physical appearance went together. Members of ethnic minorities such as the Lurs of western Iran who specialized as porters in Baghdad, for example, could be identified by a particular type of felt hat worn by men. The different Sufi orders were characterized by the style of their turbans and the folds of their gowns. Reforming

The virtuous woman

'The morals and manners of the Muslim woman are quite different from those of non-Muslim women and the women of the time of the *jahiliya*. The Muslim woman is chaste, dignified, self-respecting and modest, while the woman who is ignorant of the divine guidance may be vain, showy, and anxious to display her attractions. Such display includes exposing the attractive parts of the body, walking and talking in a seductive manner, displaying her ornaments, wearing revealing and sexy clothes, and the like.'

Qaradawi, 163.

autocrats in the nineteenth and twentieth centuries often attempted to eliminate local allegiances by insisting on standardized headgear. The best-known example was the Ottoman Fez (a red brimless felt hat worn by men) – introduced in the 1820s in the teeth of religious opposition, only to become identified in the course of a century, with 'Islamic' rectitude. Where men were ordered to change their dress to conform to ideas of progress held by Muslim rulers, upper-class Muslim women tended to adopt European dress voluntarily, by imitating the fashions imported from Europe. The exception was in Iran, where Reza Shah Pahlavi, an illiterate Cossack sergeant who rose to become the country's ruler in the 1920s, actually ordered his female subjects to remove their *chadors* (veils).

The standardized 'Islamic' dress worn by women in an increasing number of Muslim cities has no particular historical precedents, although it conforms in a general way to ideas of female modesty extrapolated from the Quran. Known as the *ziy shari'* and the *hijab* (veil), these tent shaped robes with nun-like wimples covering the head are designed to conceal both hair and feminine curves and are claimed by

Avoiding the infidel

'The Quran, the Sunna and the consensus of Muslim scholars all teach Muslims to be distinct from non-believers and in general to avoid resembling them. Anything which is likely to cause corruption in a hidden and diffuse manner is related to this matter and is likewise prohibited. The imitation of the appearance of the non-believers will lead to imitation of their immoral behaviour and evil qualities – indeed, even of their beliefs. Such influences can neither be brought under control nor easily detected, and consequently it becomes difficult or even impossible to eradicate them.'

Kitab iqtida al-sirat al-mustaqim, cited in Qadarawi, 95.

their wearers to be similar to the costumes worn by Muhammad's wives (who are ordered to protect themselves from 'behind the veil or curtain' in the only Quranic reference to female seclusion). This invented Muslim tradition first made its appearance among the female affiliates of the Muslim Brotherhood (the Muslim Sisters) during the 1930s. It became increasingly popular during the 1970s and 1980s, and generally signals support among the women wearing it for the aims of the Islamist movements. Several analysts insist adoption of the *hijab*, far from signalling the internalization by women of patriarchal attitudes, may actually represent the contrary, facilitating a new social and spatial mobility, allowing women to 'invade' public spaces previously reserved for men. By adopting 'Islamic dress' – it is argued – a woman may even defy patriarchal authority while making it plain to the non-*mahram* males she encounters of necessity outside the home that she is not sexually available, and that harassing her is tantamount to a sacrilegious act. The authority to which she considers herself answerable is no longer that of her father or brother, but that of God or perhaps the religious leader who claims to speak on his behalf. This view, however, is

9. The tent-like *burqa*, completely covering her body, through which an Afghan woman surveys the world. Displacement following on decades of war has increased pressures for female segregation and seclusion.

far from being universally accepted, and there are studies which show that the women who adopt the *hijab* are less likely than unveiled women to seek work outside the home or to be involved in higher education. In principle there is a world of difference between the situation facing women who adopt the 'veil' voluntarily and those who do so as a result of legislation. The former are exercising freedom of choice, the latter are having their freedom to choose taken away. In reality the situation is a good deal more complex than suggested by either of these alternatives. In both Muslim and non-Muslim countries the veil has become a symbolic marker of cultural identity, a shibboleth by which the Muslim woman is seen to proclaim her religious and political allegiance. In countries, including the Western diaspora, where other choices are possible, such an act can be a gesture of independence signalling a rejection of the prevailing, non-Muslim social mores. At Grenoble in France a secondary school pupil who refused to remove her head-covering even for physical education classes became at once a national heroine and national pariah: 'France is my freedom, so is my veil!' she proclaimed. Often as not, however, such choices will involve a degree of pressure, from families, husbands, or peers. The semiotics of veiling vary from region to region, city to city, *dar al-islam* to *dar al-harb*. There are no generalizations that can safely be applied 'across the board'.

Legal Reforms and the Backlash against them

In recent decades, under pressure from reformers, attempts have been made to rectify some of the legal inequalities facing women – for example, by restricting the right of unilateral divorce, or requiring that a wife register her permission with the court before her husband avails himself of the right to additional wives. Several countries have raised the minimum age of marriage. Nowadays it generally stands at 18 for boys, varying from 15 to 18 for girls, depending on the country. After the Iranian Revolution of 1979, however, the victorious clergy abolished the Family Protection Law introduced by the Shah, which set the age of marriage at 18 for girls and boys, restoring the minimum to 15 for boys and 9 for girls.

Lowering the age of marriage is evidently designed to strengthen the patriarchal family against the pressures of individualism since parents are able to exercise more influence on younger people, especially girls, in their choice of marriage partners. At the same time established social networks are breaking down under the pressures of rapid urbanization and economic change: everywhere women are exposed to encounters with men outside their *mahram* groups, encounters still deemed by many to be fraught with sexual danger. Governments, such as that of Pakistan, have responded to populist demands for a 'return' to the Shari'a by enacting laws which introduce Shari'a penalties. In 1979 the military government of General Zia ul Haqq introduced the Hudood Ordinance prescribing the Quranic punishments for *zina*, theft, drinking, and false accusations of *zina*. By insisting on Quranic standards of proof the Ordinance makes it difficult for a woman to bring charges of rape without risking a counter-accusation of *zina*, with the rules of evidence weighted against her. The safeguards are such, however, that no thief has had his hand amputated. In Sudan, by contrast, where Shari'a law has been applied to non-Muslims contrary to tradition, amputations have been applied to non-Muslims as well as Muslims convicted of theft.

Islam and Feminism

Muslim feminists argue that it is not Islam as such, but rather reactionary male interpretations of the faith that are invoked to justify patriarchal attitudes. As suggested earlier the logic of this position inevitably comes up against certain discriminatory provisions in the divine text of the Quran. A modernist hermeneutic stating that the Quranic provisions are time-contingent rather than absolute becomes necessary before the contradiction between the spiritual and moral equality of women and their legal inequality can be resolved. The argument that a woman giving evidence on a business matter might need assistance from her friend might make sense under pre-modern conditions when most women were illiterate, but as the Quranic rules stand, the testimony of a woman with a higher degree in business administration is only worth half that of an illiterate male. Beyond such textual sticking points, however, there are areas where masculine or androcentric interpretations are being contested, particularly in the field of hadith, where the questioning of sources belongs to a time-honoured methodology and is less controversial than taking issue with the text of the Quran. The biggest obstacles facing Muslim feminists are cultural and historical: feminism is perceived as coming from a hostile source.

One strategy for defusing the accusation that the Muslim feminist critic of Islamic attitudes is simply a Western-inspired lackey is the 'indigenous feminist' approach adopted by several women writers, notably the Moroccan Fatima Mernissi and the Egyptian-born Leila Ahmed. Both writers see a contradiction between the ethical principles of Islam with its commitment to social justice regardless of gender and the restrictions to which Muslim women became increasingly subjugated. For Ahmed the practices sanctioned by Muhammad in the first Muslim society reflect far more positive attitudes than became current during the later 'Abbasid era, when the practice of concubinage, sanctioned if not encouraged by Islam, became widespread. She believes that if the ethical voice of Islam had been attended to, it would have significantly tempered the 'extreme androcentric bias' of the law. Access to slaves and concubines led to women being treated as commodities, as upper-class women became increasingly marginalized. Mernissi, adopting a similar line of argument, claims that the women of the Prophet's day were relatively free. They participated with men in the public domain, if not in battle, and were active in the early Islamic movement. According to the majority of traditions, Khadija, Muhammad's trusted wife, was the 'first Muslim', the first in Muhammad's household to accept that Muhammad's messages came

Two voices

'There appear . . . to be two distinct voices within Islam, and two competing understandings of gender, one expressed in the pragmatic regulations for society . . . the other in the articulation of an ethical vision. Even as Islam instituted marriage as a sexual hierarchy in its ethical voice – a voice virtually unheard by rulers and lawmakers – it insistently stressed the importance of the spiritual and ethical dimensions of being and the equality of all individuals. While the first voice has been extensively elaborated into a body of political and legal thought, which constitutes the technical understanding of Islam, the second – the voice to which ordinary believing Muslims, who are essentially ignorant of the details of Islam's technical legacy, give their assent – has left little trace on the political and legal heritage of Islam. The unmistakable presence of ethical egalitarianism explains why Muslim women frequently insist, often inexplicably to non-Muslims, that Islam is not sexist. They hear and read in its sacred text, justly and legitimately, a different message from that heard by the makers and enforcers of orthodox, androcentric Islam.'

Ahmed, *Women and Gender in Islam*, 65–6.

from God. After her death Muhammad married many women, some of them for political reasons, others apparently for love. His favourite wife ʿAisha, daughter of his close companion Abu Bakr became the source of numerous hadiths. She was a major political actor in the civil war or strife (*fitna*) following the assassination of the third caliph ʿUthman in 656. Her role as a source of hadiths is so important that in one tradition the Prophet is supposed to have told the Muslims that they 'received half their religion from a woman'. Mernissi documents personal tensions between ʿAisha and Abu Huraira, a Companion of the Prophet who heads a great many chains of hadith transmitters, seeing in him the source of numerous anti-feminist hadiths that eventually gained currency. Mernissi's method, as Andrew Rippin points out, shares with that of the Islamists a tendency towards the remythologization of society, with both sides selectively citing the evidence to suit their arguments.

Conclusion

The symbolism conveyed by veiling may be ambiguous, but there can be no doubt that Muslim women are becoming a force to be reckoned with in the public domain. Even Saudi Arabia, bastion of Islamic sexual apartheid, has witnessed a public demonstration by women protesting against Shariʿa rulings forbidding them to drive motor vehicles. Among the less affluent, labour migration forces changes in the sexual division of labour, with a significant proportion of households now headed by women. The universities are producing more and more female graduates. Challenges to religiously grounded restrictions are inevitable. The signs of change are already apparent. The female vote is reported to have contributed substantially to the unexpected election of Muhammad Khatami to the Iranian presidency in May 1997, on a platform that included an easing of restrictions on women and greater female participation in management of the economy and state.

Chapter 6
The Two Jihads

Introduction

Jihad, like the word *fatwa*, is an Islamic term that has entered the contemporary lexicon, not least because of its use by modern Islamist movements, some of which have been actively involved in terrorism, kidnapping and other violent activities. In its primary meaning the word means 'exertion' or 'struggle', and its use in the traditional Islamic discourse is very far from being confined to military matters. The usual translation 'holy war' is therefore misleading. Many forms of activity are included under the term. In the classical formulations the believer may undertake jihad 'by his heart; his tongue; his hands; and by the sword' – the foremost of these being the first.

Jihad is collective obligation for Muslims – a duty known as *fard kifaya*, distinct from the purely personal obligations of prayer, fasting, and pilgrimage. It can be undertaken by the ruler on behalf of the whole community – and thus becomes, in the course of time, an instrument of policy. The classical doctrine of jihad was formulated during the centuries of conquest, when the faith sustained an outward momentum unprecedented in human history. The doctrine was both an expression of Islamic triumphalism and an attempt, comparable to the concept of the just war in Roman law, to limit the consequences of war. Adapting the customs of pre-Islamic bedouin warfare, an element of chivalry was built into the code: women and children, the old and the sick, were to be spared. Polytheists were faced with the choice of conversion or death, but the Peoples of the Book – initially Jews and Christians, later extended to Zoroastrians, Hindus, and others – were to be protected in return for payment of taxes (the *jizya*, a poll tax, and the *kharaj*, a tax on land). In some commentaries, the *dhimmis* (as the protected minorities are called) are to be deliberately humiliated when paying the tax. Though justified by the argument that the *dhimmis* are exempt from military duties and from the payment of *zakat*, the *jizya* is also, like the rules of marriage, an example of Islamic supremacism. This is not religious tolerance in accordance with the values of post-Enlightenment liberalism. But it falls short of the position necessary to sustain the charge that Islam 'converts by the sword'. Polytheists get short shrift, and there is no question that in parts of Africa and Asia today people adhering to animist cults have been subject to forcible Islamization. By the standards of medieval Europe, however, the doctrine of jihad is a good deal more humane than papal bulls urging the extirpation of heretics. The People of the Book who accept Islamic rule are allowed to practise their religion freely, and, since Islam defines religion in broadly orthopraxist terms, this meant in practice that religious minorities enjoyed a limited form of self-government. The Islamic record of tolerance in pre-modern times compares very favourably with that of the medieval Church.

Nevertheless the classical doctrine, as interpreted politically, does imply that Islam will ultimately prove victorious. Following the logic of jihad the world is divided into two mutually hostile camps: the sphere of Islam (*dar al-islam*) and the sphere of War (*dar al-harb*). Enemies will convert, like the polytheists, or submit, like the Christians and Jews. Those who die in 'the path of God' are instantly translated to paradise, without waiting for the resurrection or judgement day. They are buried where they fall, their bodies spared the ritual of cleansing in a mosque. The martyrs are pure already.

Just as the first Christians were obliged to postpone, indefinitely, the second coming of Christ, so the global triumph of Islam had to be deferred. The outward momentum of conquest was checked – before Constantinople, at Poitiers, and in India. The divinely appointed order came up against the intransigence of historical reality. Formerly Muslim territories such as Sicily and Spain reverted to unbelief. In due course the concept of *dar al-islam* was modified. As the divine law was communal, rather than territorial, in its application, the scholars disputed amongst themselves about the number of Muslims required to make a territory *dar al-islam*. Must the Muslims have political control, or was it merely a matter of their right to proclaim the message of Islam and to perform their religious duties? As with so many questions of law, there were no conclusive answers. The jurists disagreed about whether a particular territory was *dar al-islam* or *dar al-harb* – or in a state of suspended warfare indicated by such intermediate categories such as *dar al-sulh* (sphere of Truce).

The Greater Jihad

According to a well-known hadith, the Prophet distinguished between the 'lesser' jihad of war against the polytheists and the 'greater' jihad against evil. At its broadest, the latter was the struggle in which the virtuous Muslim was engaged throughout his or her life. Despite the *élan* of the early conquests, historically it was the 'greater' jihad which sustained the expansion of Islam in many parts of the world. The dualism of good versus evil, *dar al-islam* against *dar al-harb*, was maintained less by territorial concepts than by legal observance. *Dar al-islam* was where the law prevailed. In pre-colonial times, before the military might of the West erupted into Muslim consciousness, that law was commensurate with civilization itself. The high culture of Cairo and Baghdad extended via the trade routes to southern Africa, northern India, and south-east Asia.

The process of expansion was organic and self-directing. Since there was no church or overarching religious institution, there was no

10. The Great Mosque of Niono, Mali. Patterns of mosque design proliferated as Islam spread into different cultural regions, absorbing local vernaculars and providing opportunities for collective artistic achievements of the highest order.

universal, centrally directed missionary effort. There was, however, the demonstration effect of Muslims living literate, orderly, and sober lives. The travels of Ibn Battuta attest to the exuberant variety of a world bound together by a common faith in God and his Prophet and a common holy book and, to a lesser degree, by common practices, as well as to the prestige of its high culture. When the famous traveller from Tangier found himself in the Maldive islands, he was automatically expected to undertake the office of *qadi* because of his knowledge of the law.

The Sufi *Tariqas*

This self-same process of organic expansion along the trade routes, or among semi-settled pastoralists, was sustained by the Sufi *tariqas*, the 'mystical orders' of Islam. As we saw in Chapter 3, the Sufi adepts were engaged in ascetic and mystical practices aimed at releasing their minds from worldly attachments and eventually achieving the state of union

11. The Islamic Society of America's mosque near Indianapolis, Indiana. There may be as many as eight million Muslims in the United States. If numbers continue to grow at the current rate Islam may soon displace Judaism as the country's largest non-Christian religion.

or 'abiding' with God. The same religious impulses are found in many places, from India to western Asia and North Africa. In Christianity they find expression among individual pietists as well as in the vast and variegated traditions of monasticism. In Islam mystical practices follow the same developmental logic as oral scriptures. Just as every hadith is supplied with a line of transmitters (*isnad*) tracing it back to the Prophet, so the different Sufi disciplines or rules (Arab. *tariqa*, literally 'path') are provided with a chain (*silsila*) of authorities extending back to the Prophet, his earliest Companions, and the eponymous founders of the various orders. From the mid-twelfth century until modern times the Sufi brotherhoods flourished all over the Islamic world, from rural outbacks to the dense human fabric of the cities. It would be wrong to see the Sufis as necessarily 'withdrawn' from the world. Although some of the Sufi brotherhoods indulged in ritual practices regarded with hostility by the ʿulama, the majority insisted that inner reality of Islam (*haqiqa*) could only be approached through observance of Shariʿa, the outward or exoteric law. Under the umbrella of their different *tariqas* the

120

The traveller

Muhammad ibn ʿAbdulla ibn Battuta (1304–77) travelled for quarter of a century after making the pilgrimage to Makka, visiting Anatolia, Constantinople, Persia, the Crimea, India, and China. In the Maldive islands he reluctantly accepted the post of judge or *Qadi*. The following is an extract from his account:

'The people of the Maldive Islands are upright and pious, sound in belief and sincere in thought; their bodies are weak, they are unused to fighting, and their armour is prayer. Once when I ordered a thief's hand to be cut off, a number of those in the room fainted. The Indian pirates do not raid or molest them, as they have learned from experience that anyone who seizes any- thing from them speedily meets misfortune. In each island of theirs there are beautiful mosques and most of their buildings are made of wood ... Their womenfolk do not cover their hands, not even their queen does so, and they comb their hair and gather it to one side. Most of them wear only an apron from their waists to the ground, the rest of their bodies being uncovered. While I held the qadiship there I tried to put an end to this practice and ordered them to wear clothes, but I met with no success. No woman was admitted my presence in a lawsuit unless her body was covered, but apart from that I was unable to effect anything.'

From *Ibn Battuta Travels in Asia and Africa: 1325–1354*, tr. H. A. R. Gibb (New York, 1929), 241 ff.

brotherhoods developed formidable organizations bound by personal ties of allegiance to their leaders. The common spiritual disciplines of the orders, the gradations of spiritual authority linking the leader with his followers, the leader's intercessionary powers with God and duty of

12. Dancing Sufis from a seventeenth-century Turkish book. The 'Whirling Dervishes' hope to achieve a state of ecstasy or higher spiritual consciousness by ritualized spinning to music.

obedience owed to him: all of these made the *tariqas* important sources of social and hence political power – especially in peripheral areas such as the central Asian steppes, the Sahel, and tropical parts of Africa. Even at the centres of empire the orders were sometimes seen as a threat: for example by the Ottoman Sultan Mahmud II, who suppressed the Bektashi order in 1826.

Jihad and Resistance

The strife against evil, the 'greater jihad', might take a purely moralistic form; but at times of increasingly traumatic historical crisis, the 'lesser jihad' came to the fore. The two jihads were interchangeable. The most active movements of resistance to European rule during the nineteenth and early twentieth centuries were led or inspired by renovators (*mujaddids*), most of them members of Sufi orders, who sought to emulate the Prophet's example by purifying the religion of their day and waging war on corruption and infidelity. Such movements included the rebellion led by Prince Dipanegara in Java (1825–30), the jihad preached among the Yusufzai Pathans on the Northwest Frontier of India by Sayyid Ahmad Barelwi in 1831, the Naqshabandi Chechen leader Shamil's campaign against the Russians in the Caucasus (1834–59), and ʿAbd al-Qadir's jihad against the French in Algeria (1839–47). Not all of these movements were directed at resisting Europeans: the Mahdi Muhammad ibn Abdullah in the Sudan originally campaigned against the imperial ambitions of the Egyptians or 'Turks' he believed had abandoned Islam to foreigners ; the 'New Sect' in China, led by another Naqshbandi sheikh Ma Ming Hsin, was behind a series of major revolts against the Sinicizing policies of the Manchu emperors during the nineteenth century.

Reformists and Modernists

Once it became clear that Muslim arms were no match for the overwhelming technical and military superiority of the Europeans or nominally Muslim governments backed by them, the movement for Islamic renewal took an intellectually radical turn. Among the élites which had been exposed most directly to the European presence, the catastrophic failure of Islam was seen to lie as much in education and culture as in military defeat. A return to the pristine forms of Islam would not be enough to guarantee the survival of Islam as a civilization and way of life. The more sophisticated renovators may be divided very broadly into reformists and modernists. Reformists usually came from the ranks of the ʿulama and were more concerned with religious renewal from within the tradition. One of their most influential reformist centres was the college of Deoband in northern India, founded in 1867. The Deobandis not only attacked the cult of saints or 'friends', widespread in India, with much overlapping between Islamic and Hindu styles of devotion. They adopted a modernist stance in emphasizing personal responsibility in observance of the Shariʿa. They made full use of modern techniques of communication, including the printing press, the postal service and the expanding railway network. Deoband contributed significantly to the emergence of India's Muslims as a self-conscious community. Unlike the modernists, however, the Deobandis tried to have as little as possible to do with the British or their government. 'To like and appreciate the customs of the infidels', wrote a leading Deobandi *'alim*, Maulana Asraf 'Ali Thanawi, 'is a grave sin.' In the rural areas which were harder for them to reach their work would eventually be complemented by the Tablighi Jama'at founded by a graduate of Deoband, Maulana Muhammad Ilyas (1885–1944).

Modernism was the doctrine of the political élites and intelligentsias which had most exposure to European culture. They recognized that in order to regain political power Muslims would have to adopt European military techniques, modernize their economies and administrations, and introduce modern forms of education. On the religious front they argued for a new hermeneutic or reinterpretation of the faith in the light of modern conditions. The modernists' fascination with Europe and its works often led them to adopt Western clothes and Western lifestyles which in due course separated them from the more traditionally minded classes. It was from modernist circles that veil-ripping feminists and the leaders of nationalist movements tended to be drawn.

There are no clear lines dividing the two tendencies, which merge and divide according to circumstance. Leaders of both currents such as Sir Sayyid Ahmad Khan, founder of the Anglo-Oriental College (later University) of Aligarh in India, and reformers like Muhammad 'Abduh (d. 1906) founder of the Salafiyya movement in Egypt, tended to be found in the cultural centres of the Muslim world that had been most exposed to Western influences. Their problem was not, as 'Abduh's patron Lord Cromer (virtual ruler of Egypt between 1883 and 1907) would argue, that Islam was beyond reform; but rather that there was no institutional hierarchy comparable to that of the Christian churches through which theological and legal reforms could be effected. Reformist ʿulama like ʿAbduh or his more conservative disciple Rashid Rida had no special authority through which they could impose their views and many of their peers among the ʿulama remained unreconstructed traditionalists up till the present.

Sayyid Ahmed Khan

The most influential modernist thinker to appear in nineteenth-century India was Sir Sayyid Ahmed Khan (1817–98), founder of the Muhammadan Anglo-Oriental College at Aligarh where modern arts and sciences were taught, in English, alongside traditional Islamic studies. A former employee of the East India Company, his aim was to produce an élite of educated Muslims able to compete with Hindus for jobs in the Indian administration. Survival lay in modernizing Islamic thought and institutions. Exercising personal *ijtihad* based on a study of the Quran's Arabic idiom, Sayyid Ahmed Khan made a fundamental distinction between the details of revelation (*furuʿ*) which, he argued, referred to specific historical circumstances, and the general principles (*ʿusul*) underlying them. In principle, he believed that the laws of God as revealed through the Shariʿa were identical with the laws of nature, since the Final Cause or Creator God ultimately determined the causal relationships governing all material and non-material things.

The End of the Caliphate

On 11 November 1914 the Ottoman Sultan and Caliph Mehmet V declared a jihad or holy war against Russia, France, and Great Britain, announcing that it had become an obligation for all Muslims, whether young or old, on foot or mounted, to support the struggle with their goods and money. The proclamation, which took the form of a *fatwa*, was endorsed by religious leaders throughout the Sultan's dominions. Outside the Empire, however, its effect was minimal. In Russian central Asia, French North Africa and British India the colonial authorities generally had no difficulty in finding ʿulama to publicly endorse the Allied cause. Most galling for the Sultan-Caliph, his suzerain the Sharif Hussein of Makka, Guardian of the Holy Places, refused to endorse the jihad publicly. He had already been approached by the British with a view to launching an Arab revolt against the Turks – the revolt whose success would eventually result in the Sharif's sons Feisal and Abdullah being given the British-protected thrones of Iraq and Jordan. The Arabs of Syria, Mesopotamia, Palestine, and the Hejaz preferred freedom to 'Islamic' rule, even though for many that freedom entailed the risk (soon to be realized) of a new colonialist domination under the 'infidel'. Then, as now, pan-Islamic solidarity proved an illusion.

The collapse of the Ottoman armies in 1917–18 drove the point home. A revitalized Turkish nation under Mustafa Kemal took the ultimate step of abolishing the caliphate in 1924, bringing the crisis of Islamic legitimacy to a head. Though the decision was endorsed by the Turkish National Assembly, and generally approved by Arab nations newly freed from Ottoman dominion, the move was preceded by a mass agitation by the Muslims of India protesting against the dismemberment of the Ottoman Empire and the removal of the final link between an existing Islamic state and the divine polity founded by the Prophet Muhammad.

The Quest for an Islamic State

The Khilafat Movement (as it is known) dramatized the fundamental contradiction between pan-Islamic and nationalist aspirations. In India it represented a turning point in the anti-colonialist movement, as Muslims formerly appeased by Britain's Eastern Policy favouring the Ottoman interest, joined Hindu nationalists in opposition to the Raj. That coalition proved short-lived, and the momentum generated by the khilafat movement would eventually lead to a separate political destiny for India's Muslims in the form of Pakistan.

The movement, however, evoked no response in the Arab world and above all in Turkey, where the caliphate was associated with a discredited political system. For Arab nationalists the caliphate had come to be associated with hated Ottoman rule. The Egyptian 'alim and judge, 'Ali 'Abd al-Raziq, in a highly controversial essay published in 1925 argued that the institution had no real basis in Islam. The fact that the Prophet had combined spiritual and political roles was purely coincidental; the later caliphate did not represent a true consensus of the Muslims because it was based on force. The more conservative Rashid Rida, though once a supporter of the Ottoman caliphate, accepted its demise as symptomatic of Muslim decline; and while no advocate of secularism, he saw in the Turkish National Assembly's decision a genuine expression of the Islamic principle of consultation (*shura*). The ideal caliph, according to Rida, was an independent interpreter of the Law (*mujtahid*) who would work in concert with the 'ulama. In the absence of a suitable candidate, and of 'ulama versed in the modern sciences, the best alternative was for an Islamic state ruled by an enlightened élite in consultation with the people, able to interpret the Shari'a and legislate when necessary.

The Muslim Brotherhood

Many of Rida's ideas were taken up by the most influential Sunni reform movement, the Muslim Brotherhood, founded in 1928 by Hasan al-Banna, an Egyptian schoolteacher. The brotherhood's original aims were moral as much as political: it sought to reform society by encouraging Islamic observance and opposing Western cultural influences, rather than by attempting to capture the state by direct political action. However, during the mounting crisis over Palestine during and after the Second World War the brotherhood became increasingly radicalized. In 1948 the Prime Minister Nuqrashi Pasha was assassinated by a brotherhood member and Hasan al-Banna paid with his life in a retaliatory killing by the security services the following year.

The brotherhood played a leading part in the disturbances that led to the overthrow of the monarchy in 1952 but after the revolution it came into conflict with the nationalist government of Gamal ʿAbdul Nasser. In 1954, after an attempt on Nasser's life, the brotherhood was again suppressed, its members imprisoned, exiled, or driven underground. It was during this period that the brotherhood became internationalized, with affiliated movements springing up in Jordan, Syria, Sudan, Pakistan, Indonesia, and Malaysia. In Saudi Arabia, under the vigorous leadership of Amir (later King) Faisal ibn ʿAbdul ʿAziz, the brotherhood found refuge, and political and financial support, with funds for the Egyptian underground and salaried posts for exiled intellectuals.

The New *Jahiliya*

A radical member of the brotherhood, Sayyid Qutb, executed in 1966 for an alleged plot to overthrow the Egyptian government, would prove to be the Sunni Muslim world's most influential Islamist theorist. Some of Qutb's key ideas, however, are directly attributable to the Indian scholar and journalist Abul ʿAla Maududi, whose works became available in Arabic translation during the 1950s. One of Maududi's doctrines, in particular, would have a major impact on Islamic political movements. It was the idea that the struggle for Islam was not for the restoration of an ideal past, but for a principle vital to the here and now: the vice-regency of man under God's sovereignty. The jihad was therefore not just a defensive war for the protection of the Islamic territory or *dar al-islam*. It might be waged against governments which prevent the preaching of true Islam, for the condition of *jahiliya* (the state of ignorance before the coming of Islam) was to be found currently, in the here and now.

Qutb advocated the creation of a new élite among Muslim youth who would fight the new *jahiliya* as the Prophet had fought the old one. Like

Reinterpreting Theology

The following is an extract from a document, the Fifteen Principles, Sir Sayyid submitted to the 'Ulama of Saharanpur in 1873 or 1874:

• Whichever verses of the Glorious Quran may seem to us to contradict truth or reality, there are two explanations of such a seeming contradiction: either we have made an error in understanding the meaning of these verses, or we are mistaken in our understanding of what is truth and reality. No word of any traditionist or exegete can be regarded as authentic in opposition to it – i.e. to the word of the Glorious Quran.

• In religious matters we are bound to obey the *sunna* of the Prophet and Islam, in worldly matters we are allowed to do so [but it is not binding on us]. By the word *sunna* I mean the precepts of religion, that is all.

• As to the explicitly revealed precepts in matters of religion (*din*), the binding character of such precepts is certain. But the remaining questions which are open to the exercise of independent judgment (*ijtihad* and analogical reasoning *qiyas*) are all conjectural.

• All the precepts of the religion of Islam are in conformity with nature. Were not this so, one would have to hold a blind person guilty for not seeing and a person with eyesight guilty for seeing.

• Actions that have been commanded are good in themselves and actions that have been forbidden are bad in themselves. The Prophet only informs us about their good or bad quality like a doctor who informs about the harm and benefit of [different] medicines.

From Christian W. Troll, *Sayyid Ahmad Khan: A Reinterpretation of Muslim Theology* (New Delhi: Vikas Publishing House, 1978).

the Prophet and his Companions, this élite must choose when to withdraw from the *jahiliya* and when to seek contact with it. His ideas set the agenda for Islamic radicals throughout the Sunni Muslim world. Groups influenced by them included Shukri Mustafa, a former Muslim Brotherhood activist and leader of a group known as Takfir wa Hijra ('excommunication and emigration') who followed the early Kharijis in designating grave sinners (in this case the government) as *kafirs* (infidels); Khalid Islambuli and ʿAbd al-Salaam Farraj, executed for the murder of President Anwar Sadat in October 1981; and the Hizb al-Tahrir (Liberation Party) founded in 1952 by Shaikh Taqi al-Din al-Nabahani (1910–77), a graduate of al-Azhar whose writings lay down detailed prescriptions for a restored caliphate.

The Impact of the Iranian Revolution

While Qutb's writings have remained an important influence on Islamic radicals or 'Islamists' from Algeria to Pakistan, a major boost to the movement came from Iran where the Ayatollah Khomeini came to power after the collapse of the Pahlavi regime in February 1979. During the final two decades of the twentieth century CE the Iranian Revolution remained the inspiration for Muslim radicals or 'Islamists' from Morocco to Indonesia. Despite this universalist appeal, however, the revolution never succeeded in spreading beyond the confines of Shiʿi communities and even among them its capacity to mobilize the people remained limited. During the eight-year war that followed Iraq's invasion of Iran in 1980 the Iraqi Shiʿis who form about 50 per cent of the population conspicuously failed to support their co-religionists in Iran. The revolution did spread to Shiʿi communities in Lebanon, Saudi Arabia, Bahrein, Afghanistan, and Pakistan, but generally proved unable to cross the sectarian divide. The new Shiʿi activism in these countries either stirred up sectarian conflicts or stimulated severe repression by Sunni governments (as in Iraq and Bahrein).

Within Iran the success of the revolution had rested on three factors usually absent from the Sunni world: the mixing of Shi'i and Marxist ideas among the radicalized urban youth during the 1970s; the autonomy of the Shi'i religious establishment which, unlike the Sunni 'ulama, disposed of a considerable amount of social power as a body or 'estate'; and the eschatological expectations of popular Shi'ism surrounding the return of the Twelfth Imam.

The leading Shi'i exponent of Islam as a revolutionary ideology was 'Ali Shari'ati (d. 1977), a historian and sociologist who had been partly educated in Paris. Though without formal religious training Shari'ati reached large numbers of youth from the traditional classes through his popular lectures at the Husainiya Irshad, an informal academy he established in Tehran. Shari'ati's teachings contain a rich mix of ideas in which theosophical speculations of mystics like Ibn 'Arabi and Mulla Sadra were blended with the insights of Marx, Sartre, Camus, and Fanon (whose friend Shari'ati was and whose books he translated into Persian). The result was an eclectic synthesis of Islamic and leftist ideas. God was virtually identified with the People, justifying revolutionary action in the name of Islam. An outspoken critic of those members of the clergy who acquiesced in the Shah's tyranny, Shari'ati drew a distinction between the official Shi'ism of the Safavid dynasty (1501–1722) which made Shi'ism the state religion in Iran and the 'revolutionary' commitment of such archetypical Shi'i figures as the Imams 'Ali and Hussein and Abu Dharr al-Ghifari (a Companion of the Prophet often credited with socialist principles). Shari'ati's ideas, disseminated by means of photocopies and audio tapes, provided a vital link between the student vanguard and the more conservative forces which brought down the Shah's regime. The latter were mobilized by Sayyid Ruhallah Khomeini who had come to prominence as the leading critic of Shah Mohammed Reza Pahlavi's 'White Revolution' during the early 1960s. The Shah's agricultural and social reforms threatened the interest of the religious establishment, not least because the estates from which many of the 'ulama drew their incomes were expropriated or divided up. Exiled to Najaf in Iraq, Khomeini developed his theory of government – the *Vilayet-e faqih* (jurisconsult's trusteeship) – which broke with tradition by insisting that government be entrusted directly to the religious establishment.

The Appeal of Islamism

Outside Iran, however, the factors that contributed to the Islamic revolution continue to sustain the Islamist movements, accounting for the continuing popularity of their ideologies. The collapse of communism and the failure of Marxism to overcome the stigma of 'atheism' has made Islamism seem an attractive ideological weapon against regimes grown increasingly corrupt, authoritarian, and sometimes tyrannical. The rhetoric of national liberation, appropriated by monopolist ruling parties, has become discredited as those parties have failed to address fundamental economic and structural problems, and are increasingly seen to be controlled by tribal coteries or political cliques indifferent to the needs of the majority. In countries such as Egypt and Algeria, qualified successes achieved by governments in the field of education have turned against them, as graduates from state universities have found their career opportunities blocked. As centres of opposition mosques will always enjoy a certain privileged status, and the efforts of governments to subject them to state control are usually incomplete. The mosques are not just places of worship. They provide a communications network which will always be partially independent of the state. At the same time, the new communications technologies bring the previously illiterate classes into the political process in an unprecedented way, undermining the authority of literate elites, notably the *ʿulama*. Dale Eickelman, an American anthropologist, attributes the politicization of Islam to mass education on the one hand and the decline of the *ʿulama* on the other. 'No longer do young men regard a long apprenticeship as the prerequisite to legitimize religious knowledge. Increasingly the carriers of religious knowledge are those who claim a strong Islamic commitment, as is the case with many educated urban youths. Freed from traditional patterns of learning and scholarship, which have often been compromised by state control, religious knowledge is increasingly interpreted in a directly political fashion.'

Urbanization and its Effects

As numerous studies have shown, migration from the countryside to the city often leads to an increase in religiosity, as a more intense and self-conscious style of religious observance compensates for the more

13. The logo of the Lebanese Hizbullah, the 'Party of God', reflects the blend of religion and revolutionary 'agitprop' common to most Islamist movements.

relaxed rhythms of village life. The recently urbanized underclasses are particularly susceptible to the messages of populist preachers. At the same time the Islamist movements earn respect and gratitude by providing a network of welfare services able to fill the gaps caused by government shortfalls. Restrictions on government spending imposed by the International Monetary Fund have tended to exacerbate housing and welfare problems by forcing cuts in social spending, leading to the withdrawal of the state from some areas and its replacement by Islamic welfare organizations and charitable associations. Such voluntary organizations have found generous sources of funds in Saudi Arabia and the Gulf. The Islamic financial sector, though tainted by the massive losses sustained by investors in Egypt, provides employment opportunities and an avenue for building networks of patronage, religious orthodoxy, and political mobilization able to compensate for the disappearance of older communal bonds and patronage networks. With rapid urbanization and the growth of slums and shanty-towns the old systems have ceased to function, as *shaikhs* and notables, local and party bosses, have become detached from their previous clients. The former nationalist rhetoric, whether Nasserist or Baathist, has been discredited. 'It is into this vacuum of organization and power', writes Sami Zubaida, 'that the Islamic groups have stepped to impose their authority and discipline. The organization they impose is not one of popular participation. The activists and militants remain in charge, and the common people, to whom they provide services against modest payments, are considered as subjects of ethical reform, to be converted to orthodox conformity and mobilised in political support.'

The International Dimension

Though Islamist movements have usually been inspired by local conditions, the international factors should not be ignored. Veterans of the Afghan war against the Soviet occupation formed the core of armed and trained Islamist groups in Algeria, Yemen, and Egypt. At the height of the Afghan war there are said to have been between 10,000 and

12,000 *mujahidin* from Arab countries financed from mosques and private contributions in Saudi Arabia and the Gulf states. Many of them, ironically, are reported to have been trained by the CIA. Saudi influence also operates at the religious or ideological level. Many of the Islamists active in Egypt and Algeria spent time in Saudi Arabia as teachers or exiles, where they became converted to the rigid, puritanical version of Islam practised in that country. Thus the FIS leader in Algeria, ʿAli Ben Hadj, far from operating within the regional Maliki school of jurisprudence, which allows for considerable latitude of interpretation 'in the public interest', has tried to impose the rigid tenets of the Hanbali school prevailing in Saudi Arabia on the leadership of the (now banned) FIS.

Everywhere Islamization policies, whether imposed 'from above' by governments, or applied locally 'from below', have led to restrictions on the rights of women and religious minorities as modernist interpretations have given ground to more traditionalist attitudes. The tendency to articulate political aims in Islamic terms found constituencies in newly urbanized migrants whose understandings were typically formed in rural village milieux by mullahs or ʿulama with minimal access to modernist influences. Consequently the modernist tendency which formed an important strand in the discourse of ʿAbduh, Qutb, Banna, and even (to a lesser extent) Maududi tends to wither before the traditionalism of the recently mobilized masses. This has by no means happened everywhere, however. In central Asia the people generally rejected the 'Islamist' alternative after the collapse of the Soviet Union, despite a resurgence of Islamic activity among the young and a revival of Islamic education in schools and colleges. While Russian manipulation partly accounted for the return of the old communist *nomenklaturas* under new nationalist labels, it is also clear that in societies where literacy is universal a consensus in favour of Islamic forms of government is conspicuously absent.

The Problem of Modernization

In the Muslim heartlands, as Olivier Roy has pointed out, modernization has already occurred, but it has not been absorbed within a commonly recognized and accepted conceptual framework. It has happened 'through rural exodus, emigration, consumption, the change in family

The Tyranny of Materialism

'The Europeans worked assiduously to enable the tide of this materialistic life with its corrupting traits and its murderous germs, to overwhelm all the Islamic lands toward which their hands were outstretched. . . . They laid their plans for this social aggression in masterly fashion, invoking the aid of their political acumen and their military predominance until they had accomplished their desire. They deluded the Muslim leaders by granting them loans and entering into financial dealings with them, making all of this easy and effortless for the economy and to flood the countries with their capital, their banks, and their companies; to take over the workings of the economic machinery as they wished; and to monopolize, to the exclusion of the inhabitants, enormous profits and immense wealth. After that they were able to alter the basic principles of government, justice, and education, and to imbue political, juridical and cultural systems with their own peculiar character in even the most powerful Islamic countries. They imported their half-naked women into these regions, together with their liquors, their theatres, their dance halls, their amusements, their stories, their newspapers, their novels, their whims, their silly games, and their vices. . . . This being insufficient for them, they founded schools, and scientific and cultural institutes in the very heart of the Islamic domain, which cast doubt and heresy into the very souls of its sons and taught them how to demean

> themselves, disparage their religion and their fatherland, divest themselves of their traditions and beliefs, and to regard as sacred anything Western in the belief that only that which had a European source could serve as a model to be emulated in this life. These schools took in the sons of the upper-class alone, and became a preserve restricted to them. The sons of this class consisted of the mighty and the ruling group, and those who would shortly hold within their grasp the keys of all important matters that would concern these nations and peoples.'
>
> Hasan al-Banna, 'Between Yesterday and Today' from *Five Tracts of Hasan al-Banna: a Selection from majmu'at rasail al imam al shahid hasan al-banna*, tr. Charles Wendell (Berkeley: University of California Press, 1979), 27–8.

behaviour (a lower birthrate) but also through the cinema, music, clothing, satellite antennas, that is, through the globalization of culture'. The resulting confusion has particularly affected the position of women, formerly the protected and symbolically 'invisible' half of traditional Muslim societies. As in most other parts of the world the global economy is breaking down old extended family structures, leading to a growing necessity for women to earn cash incomes or to increase their earnings and be recognized for their efforts. Similar considerations apply to sectarian issues. Under modern conditions sectarian or ethnic rivalries that coexisted in a rough or ritualized manner in pre-modern times acquire a murderous dimension. In marked contrast to their predecessors, modern Muslim governments have tried to enforce religious and ideological uniformity on all their citizens, regardless of religious background. The result has been a significant increase in sectarian conflicts in countries with different Muslim traditions, including Turkey and Pakistan.

The legitimacy of the territorial governments established after

The modern *jahiliya*

'A truly Islamic society is not one where people call themselves "Muslims", but the Islamic law has no status, even if prayers, fasting, and pilgrimage are practised and observed. It is also not an Islamic society in which people follow their own version of Islam, contrary to what Allah and His Messenger, peace be upon him, have prescribed and explained, and call it, for example, "progressive Islam". *Jahili* society appears in various forms, all of them in defiance of Divine Guidance . . .

'How to initiate the revival of Islam? A vanguard must set out with this determination and then keep going, marching through the vast ocean of *jahiliya* which encompasses the entire world. During its course, this vanguard, while distancing itself somewhat aloof from this all-encompassing *jahiliya*, should also retain contacts with it. The Muslims in this vanguard must know the landmarks and the milestones on the road to this goal so that they would know the starting point as well as the nature, the responsibilities, and the ultimate purpose of this long journey. Not only this, but they ought to be aware of their position *vis-à-vis* this *jahiliya* which has struck its stakes throughout the earth. They must know when to cooperate with others and when to separate from them; what characteristics and qualities they should cultivate; and with what characteristics and qualities the *jahiliya*, immediately surrounding them, is armed; how to address the people of *jahiliya* in the language of Islam; what topics and problems to discuss with them; and where and how to obtain guidance in all these matters . . . I have written Milestones for this vanguard, which I consider to be a waiting reality about to be materialized.'

From Sayyid Qutb, *Milestones*, trans. of *ma`alim fi`l tariq* by Ahmad Zaki Hammad (Indianapolis: American Trust Publications, n.d.), 9.

decolonization was always open to challenge on Islamic grounds. The new national states were imposed on societies where the culture of public institutions was weak and where ties of kinship prevailed over allegiances to corporate bodies. In most Middle Eastern countries and many others beyond the Muslim heartlands, the ruling institutions fell victim to manipulation by factions based on kinship, regional, or sectarian loyalties. Even when the army took power, as the only corporate group possessing internal cohesion, the élite corps buttressing the leadership were often drawn from a particular family, sect, or tribe. In the period following decolonization the new élites legitimized themselves by appealing to nationalist goals. Their failure to 'deliver the goods' either economically or militarily (especially in the case of the states confronting Israel, and in Pakistan, which has proved unable to recover the disputed part of Kashmir from India) led to an erosion of their popular bases and the rise of movements pledged to 'restore' Islamic forms of government after years of *jahiliya* rule.

The Failure of Islamism

Following the collapse of communism Islamism is likely to dominate the political discourse in Muslim lands for the foreseeable future. But for all the anxieties about a future 'clash of civilizations' it seems unlikely to effect significant external political change. As Roy predicts, the practical effects of Islamisation entails, not a confrontation with the West, but rather a cultural retreat into the mosque and private family space. Because the Shari'a protects the family – the only institution to which it grants real autonomy – the culture of Muslims is likely to become increasingly passive, privatized, and consumer-orientated. Yet the new technologies invade the previously sacred space of the Muslim home. It is impossible to censor satellite dishes, videos, faxes, e-mail, or access to the Internet – except in small, highly urbanized areas.

Existing Muslim states are locked into the international system. Despite the turbulence in Algeria and episodes of violence in Egypt there have been fewer violent changes of government in the Middle East since 1970 than in the preceding two decades when different versions of Arab nationalism competed for power. At the same time the political instability in Pakistan and the continuing civil war in Afghanistan indicate that 'Islam' in its current political or ideological forms is unable to transcend ethnic and sectarian divisions. The territorial state, though never formally sanctified by Islamic tradition, is proving highly resilient, not least because of the support it receives militarily and economically through the international system. For all the protests by Islamist movements that Saddam Hussein's invasion of Kuwait in August 1990 was a 'Muslim affair', the result of Operation Desert Storm (in which the Muslim armies of Egypt, Pakistan, Syria, and Saudi Arabia took part alongside those of the United States and Britain) demonstrated conclusively that where major economic and political interests are at stake, the status quo wins.

Future Prospects

In the long term the globalization of culture through the revolution in communications technology must lead to a form of secularization in Muslim societies, not least because of the increasing availability of religious and cultural choice. A significant factor will be the presence of a large and growing Muslim diaspora educated in the West and able to rediscover in Islam a *voluntary* faith freed from the imperatives of enforcement while finding an outlet for Islamic values through voluntary activity. The Isma'ili community headed by the Aga Khan offers an impressive example of how Islamic concerns for welfare and social justice can be harnessed to the ancient structure of the Imamate on the basis of esoteric understandings of Islam, in which the two jihads, the activist and the quietist, have been fused together in a dynamic combination, and charged with creative energy. Although the political currents of exoteric Islam appear to be in the ascendant, it is in the pietistic and mystical traditions that future promise lies. Both Maududi and al-Banna built pietism into their systems, believing that society must be converted before the state could be conquered. Though the militants and activists who followed them, obsessed with the corruption of governments and embittered by the appalling treatment many of them received at the hands of the police, have tended to focus on action, not least because killings and bombings are bound to attract attention in an international culture dominated by television, there is evidence that quietist versions of Islam are rapidly gaining ground. The Tablighi Jama'at, originally founded in India, has spread to more than ninety countries from Malaysia to Canada and is now becoming thoroughly internationalized. Though active in promoting the faith, it is explicitly non-political. Even within Muslim countries it effectively rejects the argument that Islam should provide the framework of political life. In the diaspora at least there is clear evidence that the formerly militant Jama'at al-Islami, is moving away from the hard political line it sustained in the past in order to attract Western converts. With globalization eroding the classic distinction between *dar al-islam* and *dar al-harb* the coming decades are likely to see a retreat from direct political action and a renewed emphasis on the personal and private aspects of faith.

For all the efforts of political Islam to conquer the state on the basis of a new collectivist ideology constructed on the ruins of Marxism-Leninism and using some of its materials, the processes of historical and technological change point remorselessly towards increasing individualism and personal choice – primary agents of secularity. While regional conflicts such as Palestine or Kashmir or a political struggle for power as in Algeria may continue to be articulated in Islamist terms, any realistic assessment of the long-term prospects for the Muslim world must include the realization that modernization is inevitable. In the long term modernization is a global process that need no longer be predicated on Western cultural hegemony. The Enlightenment has come to stay, and everybody is demanding its fruits in terms of the material benefits it offers. The problem of disentangling what is universally 'modern' from what is culturally specific to any one tradition (whether Islamic or Christian, Hindu, Buddhist, or Confucian), is far from simple. It is being addressed among others by such progressive Muslim intellectuals as Mohamed Arkoun and Hasan Hanafi. It is my own belief that, despite historical differences in the relations between the state and civil society, the Muslim world will develop along the lines previously travelled by the post-Christian West. For all the protestations to the contrary, the faith will be internalized, becoming private and voluntary. In an era when individuals are ever less bound by ties of kinship and increasingly exposed to urban anomie, Muslim souls are likely to find the Sufi path of inner exploration and voluntary association more rewarding than revolutionary politics. Sadly, more blood can be expected to be spilt along the way.

Appendix:
The Five Pillars of Islam

The basic religious duties of Muslims are known as the Five Pillars.

1. *Shahada*: declaration of faith according to the formula *There is no god but God. Muhammad is the Messenger of God.* To this the Shiʿi minority add: ʿAli is the Friend of God (see Chapter 4).

2. *Salat*: worship. Sometimes translated as 'prayer', *salat* takes the form of a ritual prostration in which the precise bodily movements are as important as the accompanying mental activity. Sunni Muslims are required to perform *salat* five times daily – at dawn, noon, mid-afternoon, sunset and evening. Worshippers must be in a state of ritual purity achieved by performing major or minor ablutions, depending on the degree of pollution brought about by bodily secretions, sexual activity, contact with animals and so forth. *Salat* may be performed virtually anywhere, provided the worshipper faces the *qıbla* – the direction of the Kaʿba in Makka. The congregational prayer is performed at noon on Fridays when all adult male members of the community are gathered. Males and females are usually separated, with women worshipping behind the men or in a screened-off section of the mosque. A sermon is usually delivered by the Imam or prayer-leader. Under the Islamic government of Iran, Friday sermons delivered by religious leaders who are also major political players are often the occasions of major policy pronouncements.

The Niceties of Fasting

'The Fast of Ramadan becomes obligatory when thirty days of the preceding month, Sha'ban are past, or with the seeing of the new moon of Ramadan. This seeing is established with the testimony of one trustworthy witness, or as some say, two. If one witness is accepted, it is a condition that he must have the quality of veracity, and thus be neither a slave nor a woman . . . To fast, one must rigorously avoid coition, vomiting . . . or introducing any substance to the "interior of the body". Some make it a condition that there be in the body power to absorb the food or the medicine thus introduced. It does not matter if the "interior" is inside the head, or the belly, or the intestines or the bladder; all can break the fast with the introduction of a substance by sniffing or eating or injection, or through incision into the belly or the head, or the like. According to the soundest opinion, putting drops in the nose or the urethra breaks the fast. It is necessary [however] for such an introduction to be by an open passage. Thus there is no harm in oils entering the pores by absorption, or when kohl (antimony) is used, and its taste is afterward perceived in the throat. The introduction must be intended, so that if a fly or gnat or dust of the road or flour-dust entered by accident, the fast would not be broken. It would also not be broken if one swallowed saliva carelessly. But the fast is broken if saliva leaves the mouth and one brings it back into the mouth, or if one moistens a thread in one's mouth and then puts it back in one's mouth still moist, or if one swallows saliva in which a foreign substance or something unclean is mixed.'

Extract from instructions on observing the fast of Ramadan
by Muhyi al-Din al-Nawawi (d. 1277) a *faqih* of the school
of Shafii.

3. *Zakat* – alms-giving/compulsory charity. This tax, payable once a year by all adult Muslims, is assessed at 2.5 per cent of capital assets over and above a minimum known as the *nisab*. For example the *nisab* for stock consists of five camels, thirty cows (including oxen and buffaloes), or forty sheep or goats. *Zakat* is payable on bank deposits, precious metals, merchandise used in trade (but not personal possessions such as cars, clothing, houses, and jewellery), livestock, and crops from tilled land. The recipients should be the poor and needy. In the past *zakat* was collected by the Muslim government and distributed according to pre-established patterns. Nowadays giving is usually left to the believer's conscience.

4. *Sawm*: the fast during Ramadan. The fast which takes place during daylight hours in the holy month of Ramadan, the ninth month of the lunar calendar, applies to eating, drinking, smoking, and sexual activity. The fast begins at dawn and ends at sunset. In Muslim countries such as Egypt the breaking of the fast at sundown is an occasion for joyful celebration, with tables laid out in the streets and feasting that carries on well into the night. A pre-fast meal is usually served before dawn. Ramadan is traditionally an occasion for both family get-togethers and religious reflection. It is considered especially meritorious to recite the whole of the Quran during the sacred month. According to tradition the Quran 'came down' on the 27 Ramadan, the 'Night of Power'.

5. *Hajj*: pilgrimage to Makka. This intense and demanding religious obligation is required of every adult Muslim at least once in his or her lifetime. The annual pilgrimage or Hajj takes place during the last ten days of the twelfth lunar month (Dhu'l al-Hijja) reaching its climax with the Feast of Sacrifice ('Id al-Adha), a festival honoured throughout the Muslim world with the slaughter of a specially fattened sheep, cow or camel in commemoration of the Sacrifice of Abraham. The minor pilgrimage or 'Umra may be performed at any time of the year. In the past Muslims from far-flung regions would spend the best part of a lifetime on the journey, working their way across Africa or Asia to reach

The Benefits of Hunger

The Imam al-Ghazali's famous spiritual manual, 'The Revival of the religious Sciences' (*Ihya 'ulum al-din*) offers a less legalistic view of fasting, emphasizing its spiritual and social virtues.

'Hunger has ten benefits. The first is the purification of the heart, the illumination of the natural disposition and the sharpening of one's insight. For satiety engenders stupidity and a blindness in the heart, and increases the vapours of the brain to produce a form of inebriation, so that the sources of thought are repressed and the heart finds it a burdensome thing to think and to perceive things with any rapidity . . . The second benefit is softness and purity of the heart by which it is readied to attain the delight of intimate discourse with God and to be affected by His remembrance . . . The third benefit lies in mortification and abasement, and the removal of exultation, rejoicing and exuberance, which comprises the beginning of rebellion and heedlessness of God (Exalted is He!). For the soul is mortified and abased by nothing more effective than hunger, which, when it prevails, causes it to have placid trust in its Lord and fear of Him, and to be aware of its helplessness and abasement when it weakens and becomes desperate for the morsel of bread which it misses, so that the whole world appears dark to a man because one drink of water did not come when he desired it . . . The fourth benefit is that one comes never to forget God's trials and torments, or those who are afflicted by them, for the man sated is liable to forget those people who are hungry and to forget hunger itself . . . The fifth and greatest benefit lies in the breaking of all one's desires for sin, and achieving mastery over the soul which commands evil. For all sin originates in one's desires and strengths, the stuff of which is food in every case: when one eats less, every one of one's

> desires and strengths will be enfeebled ... This does not con-
> stitute one single benefit; rather it is the storehouse of all bene-
> fits, for this reason it has been said that "hunger is one of God's
> storehouses".'
>
> From the 'On Breaking the Two Desires': Book 23 of the *Ihya 'ulum
> al-din*, trans. T. J. Winter, Cambridge Islamic Texts Society (1995).

the Holy City. On their return they enjoyed the honoured status of
Hajji – one who has made the pilgrimage. Nowadays the journey has
been greatly facilitated by inexpensive air transport. About two
million pilgrims perform the Hajj annually. Half of them come from
overseas. Their numbers are limited by a quota system operated by
the Saudi authorities, guardians of the Holy Places in conjunction
with Muslim governments. The arduous rituals, often performed
in the intense heat of an Arabian summer, include the Tawaf – the
circumambulation of the Ka'ba; the Sa'i (seven-fold running between
the hillocks of Safa and Marwa, now covered in an air-conditioned
gallery); the Standing in the Plain of 'Arafat, a few miles from Makka;
the 'Onrush' through the narrow defile of Muzdalifa; the 'Stoning' of
three pillars representing the devil; and the sacrifice of an animal at
Mina (formerly performed in the open, nowadays conducted in
hygienic abattoirs, with the pilgrims purchasing 'sheep certificates'
for meat that will be frozen and distributed to poor families in various
Muslim lands).

In recent years Iranian pilgrims have used the Hajj to make political
statements attacking Israel, the West, and by implication the pro-
Western Saudi dynasty, much to the annoyance of the authorities and
the majority of pilgrims who regard the Hajj as a purely religious
festival. In August 1987 the Saudis reported that 402 people, of whom
275 were Iranians, had been killed in disturbances resulting from
political demonstrations. In 1990 more than 1,100 pilgrims, mainly from

Turkey and Indonesia were crushed to death when a pedestrian bridge collapsed under the weight of people. In 1997 several hundred pilgrims, mainly from India and Pakistan, were burnt to death when fire swept through the camp at Mina.

References

All quotations from the Quran are from A. J. Arberry, *The Quran Interpreted* (London, 1955) unless indicated by *.

Chapter 1
'The clash of civilizations?': Samuel Huntington, *Foreign Affairs* (72: 3, 1993), 22–9; The myth of confrontation: Fred Halliday, *Islam and the Myth of Confrontation: Religion and Politics in the Middle East* (London, 1995), 6; 'Islamic Constitution': Sami Zubaida, *The People and the State* (London, 1993), 173; social imaginary: Mohammed Arkoun, *Rethinking Islam: Common Questions, Uncommon Answers* (tr. and ed. Robert D. Lee, Boulder, Colo., 1994), 6–13; venture of Islam: Marshall G. S. Hodgson, *The Venture of Islam: Conscience and History in a World Civilization* (3 vols., Chicago, 1974), i: *The Classical Age of Islam*, 3–99; a ruler who has no say at all: Patricia Crone and Martin Hinds, *God's Caliph: Religious Authority in the First Centuries of Islam* (Cambridge, 1986), 108–9; rise of modern political movements in Islam: Peter von Sivers in John Esposito (ed.), *The Oxford Encyclopedia of the Modern Islamic World* (4 vols., Oxford, 1995), ii. 259–60.

Chapter 2
verbal ritual enclosure: Denny, *Introduction to Islam*, 160–1, Muhammad transported by night from distant shrine: *Quran* 17: 1; acceptance of Islam: Ibn Ishaq, *The Life of Muhammad: A Translation of Ishaq's 'Sirat*

Rasul Allah' (tr. and ed. Alfred Guillaume, Oxford, 1955), 117; so-called Satanic Verses: Guillaume, ibid., 165; prosperous Jewish farms: Kitab al Aghani, in F. E. Peters, *Muhammad and the Origins of Islam* (Albany, NY, 1994), 193; vast flood of tradition: Chirag 'Ali, in Annemarie Schimmel, *And Muhammad is His Messenger* (Chapel Hill, NC, 1985), 30; no official doctrine concerning Prophet's sinlessness: Schimmel, ibid., 48; Jami, 'A little stone', in Schimmel, ibid. 76.

Chapter 3

bila kaif: I. R. Netton, *Allah Transcendent* (London, 1994), 26; orthopraxy: Julian Baldick, 'Among the Friends of God', *Times Literary Supplement* (26 Sept. 1986); remote, unknowable God: Netton, *Allah Transcendent*, 27; 'the One Reality, God': Netton, ibid., 290; 'No one expected the Hidden Imam to arrive in a Jumbo Jet!': Shariatmadari in H. M. Heikal, *The Return of the Ayatollah* (London, 1981), 177.

Chapter 4

endless debate: Norman Anderson, *Law Reform in the Muslim World* (London, 1976), 178; 'Whatever the Muslims see as good is good with God', George F. Hourani, *Islamic Law and Legal Theory* (ed. Ian Edge, Dartmouth, 1996), 161; Prophet's meeting with Mu'adh ibn Jabal: M. Bertrand in *Encyclopedia of Islam*, v. 281; *Ijtihad*: Sayf-al-Din al-Amidi in Edge, *Islamic Law and Legal Theory*, 281; 'from murder to social etiquette': J. N. D. Anderson, ibid., 88; judge's acute sense of observation: Lawrence Rosen, *The Anthropology of Justice: Law as Culture in Islamic Society* (Cambridge, 1989), 52; Islamist belief in government: Olivier Roy, *The Failure of Political Islam* (London, 1994).

Chapter 5

sleeping foetus: Leila Badawi in Jean Holm and John Bowker (eds.), *Women in Religion* (London, 1994), 94; encouragement to marry: Yusuf al-Qaradawi, *The Lawful and the Prohibited in Islam* (*al-halal wal-haram fil islam*) (tr. Kamal El-Helbawy, M. Moinuddin Siddiqui, and Syed Shukry, Indianapolis, 1985), 173; marriage and patterns of dominance: Fuad I.

Khuri, *Imams and Emirs: State, Religion and Sects in Islam* (London, 1990), 85–8; temporary marriage: Shahla Haeri, *Oxford Encyclopedia of the Modern Islamic World*, iv. 212; lyrical view of life/infinite orgasm: Abdulwahab Bouhdiba, *Sexuality in Islam* (tr. Alan Sheridan, London, 1985), ch. 7; homosexuality: Yusuf al-Qaradawi, *The Lawful and the Prohibited in Islam*, 169; beards: ibid. 94; the presence of females: Edward Lane, *An Account of the Manners and Customs of the Modern Egyptians* (London, 1836; facsimile New York, 1973), 82; Christianity and marriage: Jack Goody, *The Development of the Family and Marriage in Europe* (Cambridge, 1983); family sanctuaries: E. W. Fernea in *Oxford Encyclopedia of the Modern Islamic World*, ii. 49; Lurish hats: Freya Stark, *Letters*, ii: *The Open Door 1930–35* (1975), 54; pupil from Grenoble: Gilles Kepel, *Allah in the West* (Oxford, 1997), 226; half of religion received from a woman: Soraya al-Torki in *Oxford Encylopedia of the Modern Islamic World*, iv. 328; remythologization of society: Andrew Rippin, *Muslims: Their Religious Beliefs and Practices*, ii: *The Contemporary Period* (London, 1993), 124.

Chapter 6

'To like and appreciate the customs of the infidels is a great sin': Thanawi, in Philip Lewis, *Islamic Britain* (London, 1994), 36; reformed Islam: Earl of Cromer, *Modern Egypt* (London, 1908), ii. 184, 233; fatwa, 11 Nov. 1914: Rudolph Peters, *Islam and Colonialism: The Doctrine of Jihad in Modern History* (The Hague, 1979), 90 ff.; politicization of Islam: Dale Eickelman, in *Oxford Encyclopedia of the Modern Islamic World*, iii. 342; vacuum of organization and power: Sami Zubaida, *Islam, The People and The State: Essays on Political Ideas and Movements in the Middle East* (London, 1993), p. xvii.

Further Reading

Chapter 1

INTRODUCTORY TEXTS: Frederick Mathewson Denny, *An Introduction to Islam* (New York, 1985); Andrew Rippin, *Muslims: Their Religious Beliefs and Practices*, i: *The Formative Period* (London, 1990), ii: *The Contemporary Period* (London, 1993); Malise Ruthven, *Islam in the World* (rev. edn., London, 2000); David Waines, *An Introduction to Islam* (Cambridge, 1995). HISTORIES: Marshall G. S. Hodgson, *The Venture of Islam: Conscience and History in a World Civilization* (3 vols., Chicago, 1974); Albert Hourani, *A History of the Arab Peoples* (London, 1991); Ira Lapidus, *A History of the Islamic Peoples* (Cambridge, 1993). ENCYCLOPEDIAS/DICTIONARIES: *The Encyclopedia of Islam* (rev. edn., 6 vols., incomplete); John Esposito (ed.), *The Oxford Encylopedia of the Modern Islamic World* (4 vols., Oxford, 1995); H. A. Gibb and J. H. Kramers (eds.), *The Shorter Encyclopedia of Islam* (6 vols., Leiden, 1961) – contains no material published since 1936; Cyril Glassé (ed.), *The Encyclopedia of Islam* (London, 1990); T. P. Hughes, *A Dictionary of Islam* (1896) – available in photo reprint form Ian Netton, *A Popular Dictionary of Islam* (Curzon Press, 1997).

Chapter 2

HADITH COLLECTIONS AVAILABLE IN ENGLISH TRANSLATION: Sulayman ibn al-Ashʾath al-Sijistani Abu Daud, *Sunan Abu Dawud* (tr Ahmad Hasan, 3 vols., Lahore, 1984); Muhammad ibn Ismaʾil al-Bukhari, *Sahih al-Bukhari* (tr.

Muhammad Muhsin Khan, 9 vols., Chicago, 1979); Malik ibn Anas, *Al-Muwatta* (tr. ʿAisha ʿAbdarrahman al-Tarjumana and Yaʾcoub Johnson, Norwich, 1982); Muslim ibn Hajjaj al-Qushayri, *Al-Jamiʿ us-Sahih* (tr. William Chittick, Albany, NY, 1981). RECOMMENDED BIOGRAPHIES OF MUHAMMAD: Michael Cook, *Muhammad* (Oxford, 1983); Guillaume, *Life of Muhammad*; Maxim Rodinson, *Mohamed* (Harmondsworth, 1971); W. Montgomery Watt, *Muhammad at Mecca* (Oxford, 1953) and *Muhammad at Medina* (Oxford, 1956). TEXTUAL CRITICISM OF HADITH LITERATURE: Daniel W. Brown, *Rethinking Tradition in Modern Islamic Thought* (Cambridge, 1996). Ignaz Goldziher, *Muslim Studies* (tr. and ed. S. M. Stern, London, 1971); Joseph Schacht, *The Origins of Muhammadan Jurisprudence* (Oxford, 1950).

Chapter 3
Farhad Daftary, *The Ismaʿilis: Their History and Doctrines* (Cambridge, 1990); ʿAsgharl Farhad Daftary, *A Short History of the Ismailis* (Edinburgh, 1998). Ali Engineer, *The Bohras* (New Delhi, 1980), M. Fakhry, *A History of Islamic Philosophy* (London, 1983); Moojen Momen, *An Introduction to Shiʿi Islam* (New Haven, 1985); Yann Richard, *Shiʿite Islam* (tr. Antonia Nevill, Oxford, 1995).

Chapter 4
Norman Calder, *Studies in Early Muslim Jurisprudence* (Oxford, 1993). N. J. Coulson, *A History of Islamic Law* (Edinburgh, 1964); Wael B. Hallaq, *A History of Islamic Legal Theories* (Cambridge, 1997).

Chapter 6
Leonard Binder, *Islamic Liberalism: A Critique of Development Ideologies* (Chicago, 1988); François Burgat and William Dowell, *The Islamic Movement in North Africa* (Austin, Tex., 1993); Akbar S. Ahmed and Hastings Donnan (eds.), *Islam, Globalization and Postmodernity* (London, 1994); Akbar S. Ahmed, *Postmodernism and Islam: Predicament and Promise* (London, 1992); Daniel Easterman, *New Jerusalems: Reflections on Islam, Fundamentalism and the Rushdie Affair* (London, 1993); Ernest

Gellner, *Postmodernism, Reason and Religion* (London, 1992); Gilles Kepel, *The Prophet and Pharaoh* (London, 1982); Fatima Mernissi, *Islam and Democracy: Fear of the Modern World* (London, 1993); Olivier Roy, *The Failure of Political Islam* (tr. Carol Volk, London, 1994); Malise Ruthven, *A Satanic Affair: Salman Rushdie and the Wrath of Islam* (rev. edn. London, 1991); Emmanuel Sivan, *Radical Islam: Medieval Theology and Modern Politics* (New Haven, 1985).

Index

Index

Islam

Islam

Fundamentalism
by Malise Ruthven

Since the end of the Cold War, and especially
since 9/11, Islamic fundamentalism has come
to be viewed as the greatest threat to Western
liberal democracy. Ruthven charts the
development of various fundamentalist
movements from the 1920s in America, to the
rise of fundamentalist groups in the Middle-
East in the early 21st Century, and investigates
the many different forms of fundamentalist
belief, and the political and terrorist activities
that often result.

'Finally the first clear definition of this
indespensible, yet misused term.'

Professor Anoush Ehteshami,
University of Durham

0-19-284091-6   £12.99   April 2004

OXFORD